At Issue

The US Energy Grid

Other Books in the At Issue Series:

Are Athletes Good Role Models?

Are Natural Disasters Increasing?

The Energy Crisis

How Safe Is America's Infrastructure?

Hurricane Katrina

Is Childhood Becoming Too Sexualized?

Piracy on the High Seas

Polygamy

Should the Internet Be Free?

Should the U.S. Close Its Borders?

Should Vaccinations Be Mandatory?

Teen Smoking

What Is the Impact of E-Waste?

What Is the Impact of Tourism?

What Role Should the U.S. Play in the Middle East?

At Issue

The US Energy Grid

David Haugen, Susan Musser, and Ross M. Berger,
Book Editors

GREENHAVEN PRESS
A part of Gale, Cengage Learning

Detroit • New York • San Francisco • New Haven, Conn • Waterville, Maine • London

Elizabeth Des Chenes, *Managing Editor*

For more information, contact:
Greenhaven Press
27500 Drake Rd.
Farmington Hills, MI 48331-3535
Or you can visit our Internet site at gale.cengage.com

Articles in Greenhaven Press anthologies are often edited for length to meet page requirements. In addition, original titles of these works are changed to clearly present the main thesis and to explicitly indicate the author's opinion. Every effort is made to ensure that Greenhaven Press accurately reflects the original intent of the authors. Every effort has been made to trace the owners of copyrighted material.

LIBRARY OF CONGRESS CATALOGING-IN-PUBLICATION DATA

The US energy grid / David Haugen, Susan Musser, and Ross M. Berger, book editors.
p. cm. -- (At issue)
Includes bibliographical references and index.
ISBN 978-0-7377-5602-9 (hardcover) -- ISBN 978-0-7377-5603-6 (pbk.)
1. Power resources--United States. I. Haugen, David M., 1969- II. Musser, Susan. III. Berger, Ross M.
TJ163.25.U6U8 2012
333.793'2--dc23

2011040163

Printed in the United States of America
1 2 3 4 5 16 15 14 13 12

FD084

Contents

Introduction

On August 14, 2003, a wide-scale blackout affected more than 55 million people from Ontario, Canada, down to the Midwestern and Northeastern United States. Major cities such as New York, Cleveland, Toronto, and Baltimore had no electricity for over 24 hours and, in some areas, for more than three days. During this time, citizens in blacked-out regions were on edge. A lack of functioning streetlights meant a greater risk of traffic accidents, no air conditioning meant little relief from summer heat, and fears of looting persisted. Corporate productivity dropped. Suffering through the long hours without power, people could only wonder when—or if—their power would be restored.

Affected cities did not regain full use of their electric capacity until August 18. In the aftermath, both Canadian and American officials conducted extensive investigations to determine what happened and why it took so long to restore power to affected homes and cities. Among their findings, officials discovered that FirstEnergy Corp—a company devoted to the generation, transmission, and delivery to electricity to over 4.5 million households in the Midwestern United States—had failed to upgrade its already deteriorating system and the network failed when tree branches struck power lines in Ohio. The resulting power surge spread north and east through the interconnected energy systems, clearly proving to investigators that a power shut down originating with one company could easily impact other power companies using the same grid. In a November 20, 2003, article in the *Chicago Sun-Times*, then US Energy Secretary Spencer Abraham was quoted as stating, "A number of relatively small problems combined to become a very big one."

Although the fallout from the 2003 blackout resulted in a lot of finger-pointing, the chief concern among analysts was the composition of the US energy grid itself. This system—which interlocks various energy providers across the nation—was set up to ensure that energy providers could lend power to another part of the country if needed. Energy could be borrowed from neighboring networks or resources halfway across the country. However, what the blackout proved was that the entire grid was also at the mercy of varying standards, practices, and infrastructure in each network. Relatedly, observers continued to point out that the grid was overly reliant on fossil-fuel-burning power plants that both relied on dwindling fuel reserves and sent tons of carbon emissions into the atmosphere. Further, the energy grid, which had been conceived in the 1960s, appeared mired by corporate attitudes about production and distribution that had failed to keep pace with the changing energy picture in the twenty-first century.

Since roughly 2005, there has been an ever-increasing pressure for the adoption of a "smart grid," a re-conception of a national power grid that would increase efficiency, lower costs, and promote an eco-friendly approach to energy production and consumption. In the Green Blog of Boston.com, Beth Daley wrote on January 26, 2009, that the proposed smart grid would "use digital technology to allow two-way communication between electricity generators and customers. It will . . . allow appliances in homes to use electricity when it is abundant and inexpensive. It will allow electricity managers to peer into their systems to identify problems and avoid them. It will provide rapid information about blackouts and power quality." According to Daley, a smart system will also integrate large-scale renewable energy projects (such as solar and wind) into the existing energy grid. What's more, a smart system will apply "islanding," a concept that involves a consumer's temporary use of power from a local rooftop solar panel or other renewable energy source when there is a utility overload or failure. That way, power use can continue uninterrupted during times of a conventional outage.

This idealized grid still incorporates a cross-country network of providers and distributors, but instead of relying on a few large suppliers to meet the demands of a growing number of consumers, the smart grid will fuse local energy production (through renewables) into a system that trades power across a multitude of suppliers. Thus, consumers will be able to draw power from national grids as well as from their own wind turbine or a neighbor with a solar panel. Smart grid enthusiasts fully expect that many consumers will become producers of energy, allowing for a more dispersed and reliable chain of supply and distribution. The new grid will also employ smart meters in homes and businesses to regulate power use and avoid waste. Such a change in infrastructure will not be cheap, nor will it arrive soon. According to a May 2011 report by the Electric Power Research Institute entitled "Estimating the Costs and Benefits of the Smart Grid: A Preliminary Estimate of the Investment Requirements and the Resultant Benefits of a Fully Functioning Smart Grid," the cost to upgrade the current US power grid ranges from $338 to $476 billion—and that's more than a 100 to 188 percent increase from a 2004 forecast.

Opponents of the smart grid believe that the modernization of the current power system would be disruptive. They also point out that among smart grid advocates, there seems to be a prevailing assumption that consumers will adopt a completely green life to reap the maximum benefits of a smart grid, such as the purchase of an electric car that can act as a back-up power supply for a home experiencing an outage. Few American families are financially equipped to adopt such expensive technologies, especially when the practical and money-saving aspects of conversion have not been tested on a grand scale. In an April 27, 2009, *Wall Street Journal* article about the potential use of home smart meters, Rebecca Smith wrote that "consumer advocates fear the costs could be greater than the savings for many households." Smith argues that this is a valid concern considering that power companies will require residential consumers to buy these devices, which can potentially cost $250 to $500.

However, advocates of smart meters believe that, despite the initial cost, consumers will save more money in the long run. Smart meters help consumers by steadily monitoring their energy consumption and its cost. By helping consumers minimize their consumption during peak hours, smart meters can help consumers achieve significant savings. The state of California reports that nearly 5.3 million smart meters have been installed throughout the state's residences and commercial properties. Moreover, according to the California Public Utilities Commission website, "Smart Meters enable a utility to measure a customer's electricity usage in hourly increments." Such a benefit allows a customer to exercise greater control over their electricity use by choosing a pricing plan more appropriate to their needs. This is the ultimate goal of smart grid promoters—giving consumers more choice in how they use electricity and making the system more democratic and sustainable.

Supporters of this kind of change believe that the smart grid is the future because it takes into account the inevitable decline of fossil fuels while stressing personal responsibility and sustainable living. They also insist the growth in smart grid jobs is an added perk of a green economy. According to the National Commission on Energy Policy's 2009 study "Task Force on America's Future Energy Jobs," the upgrading of the US energy grid "will require not only new, low-carbon technologies and systems, but people with the expertise to create those technologies and to plan, design, build, operate, and maintain those technologies and systems." During a time of economic uncertainty, the smart grid appears to offer a new avenue of investment and employment.

The promise of a smart grid may be enormous, yet its potential payoff is still uncertain. The viewpoints in *At Issue: The*

US Energy Grid offer differing opinions on the feasibility, expense, and utility of changing the way power is delivered in the United States. Some believe conversion to a smart grid is a necessary gamble; others caution the technology and practicality of the proposed system are simply at odds with the power demands and financial strength of the nation. No one wishes to experience another power outage the size of the 2003 blackout, but the adoption or dismissal of a smart grid are equally unproven methods of preventing another such catastrophe.

1

A Smart Energy Grid Will Revolutionize Energy Production and Distribution

Chioke Harris and Jeremy P. Meyers

Chioke Harris is a graduate student in mechanical engineering at the University of Texas in Austin. He researches large-scale energy storage and energy modeling. Jeremy P. Meyers is an assistant professor of mechanical engineering at the University of Texas in Austin.

While the current electrical grid in the United States has not changed in more than fifty years, coming improvements will transform the system greatly. The new model will be a "smart grid," a transmission and distribution network that will link energy providers, storage facilities, and consumers in unique ways. Smart energy meters will allow providers to monitor and counsel consumers on energy use, and energy saving technologies employed in businesses and in the home will also regulate energy use. The idea is to create communication between supplier and user to make energy use more efficient, less costly, and less wasteful. The smart grid will incorporate renewable energy resources and storage facilities to meet the nation's demands without sacrificing service. Overall, the new system will revolutionize power supply and consumption in the twenty-first century.

Chioke Harris and Jeremy P. Meyers, "Working Smarter, Not Harder: An Introduction to the 'Smart Grid,'" *Interface*, Fall 2010. pp. 45–48.

Consider, for a moment, how communications have changed in the latter half of the 20th century through the first decade of the 21st. In the span of a few decades, we have progressed from rotary-dial telephones and expensive long-distance calling to the Internet, e-mail, cell phones, videoconferencing, IP [Internet protocol] telephony, and video chats. We are more connected to information and to distant people and places than ever before.

Now consider how our relationship to the electric grid has changed over that same time period. Odds are, you still plug your appliances into an AC [alternating current] outlet, and the way that the power is generated and brought to your home or office doesn't significantly affect how you consume that power.

[T]he slow pace of innovation and change on the electric grid is about to change with the introduction of the smart grid.

Old vs. New Energy Grids

The development of the electrical grid has been one of the key technical advancements of the 20th century. Both its scale and the scope of its distribution speak volumes about how important it has become to modern life. The modern grid, however, is still largely based on the original design that [George] Westinghouse and [Thomas] Edison debated in the late 1800s, and isn't designed for modern electrical loads, distributed energy sources, or optimal efficiency. Power is generated and distributed by utility companies, without local competition to speak of, and with fairly little communication between utilities and end users in terms of how to get more out of the system. To date, the revolutions that we have seen in communications have very few analogs in the electric grid.

Nearly all the existing electric transmission and distribution infrastructure in the United States was built prior to 1965. Since then, that system has had five major outages. While this may seem like an impressive track record, three of the five outages have occurred in the past decade. Every year, American businesses lose an estimated $100 billion as a result of power quality problems and blackouts. Nonetheless, it took the massive blackout across the northeastern United States and southeastern Canada in 2003, which resulted in a loss of $6 billion in economic productivity, to place in sharp focus the need to reinvest in transmission infrastructure.

By all accounts, however, the slow pace of innovation and change on the electric grid is about to change with the introduction of the smart grid. Precise definitions of what comprises the smart grid can vary, but generally speaking, this term refers to the use of digital information and controls technology to improve the reliability, security, and overall efficiency of the electric grid. Proponents suggest that this will be accomplished by offering consumers and utilities incentives to work together to create a more responsive and less polluting system.

A popular description of the smart grid invokes the idea of an "energy Internet" with a two-way flow of energy, in much the same way that the Internet allowed greater interactivity and selectivity in the flow of information. Just as we have seen television programming move away from broadcast to cable to video-on-demand and DVR [digital video recorder] technology, proponents of the smart grid imagine that we will see energy flow onto and off the grid as customer and utility exchange information, a marked contrast from today's one-way, utility-to-customer energy system.

A More Efficient System

Broadly speaking, the smart grid is a fusion of the information technology that has enabled mobile telephony and the

Internet with our existing electric grid. In addition to improvements in system resiliency and responsiveness to outages, the smart grid will also enable greater system efficiency, increased installation of wind and solar energy and active participation of consumers in managing their electricity use. The Electric Power Research Institute (EPRI) has found that rollout of smart grid technologies could yield a 4% reduction in energy use by 2030. As a point of comparison, that would be roughly equivalent to eliminating the emissions of 750 million cars. Beyond the emissions impact, that translates to a $20.4 billion in annual savings for utility customers nationwide. With a more robust and efficient system, and better knowledge and control of demand, it will be easier for utilities to manage the integration of renewable energy sources that produce intermittent power. That will help states meet targets for renewable power growth and minimize fuel consumption by reducing their dependence on natural gas or diesel reserve generators and use of fossil fuel-based power plants.

While smart grid technologies have been studied and piloted by the Department of Energy (DOE), universities and research organizations, in regards to federal support, the specific functions and features of the smart grid are explicitly defined by Title XIII of the Energy Independence and Security Act (EISA).

In addition to improvements in system resiliency and responsiveness to outages, the smart grid will also enable greater system efficiency, increased installation of wind and solar energy and active participation of consumers in managing their electricity use.

As defined by Title XIII, specific features of the smart grid are:

- increased use of digital information and controls technology to improve reliability, security, and efficiency of the electric grid;

- dynamic optimization of grid operations and resources, with full cyber-security;
- deployment and integration of distributed resources and generation, including renewable resources;
- deployment of "smart" technologies (real-time, automated, interactive technologies that optimize the physical operation of appliances and consumer devices) for metering, communications concerning grid operations and status, and distribution automation;
- integration of "smart" appliances and consumer devices;
- deployment and integration of advanced electricity storage and peak-shaving technologies, including plug-in electric and hybrid electric vehicles, and thermal-storage air conditioning;
- development of standards for communication and interoperability of appliances and equipment connected to the electric grid, including the infrastructure serving the grid; and
- identification and lowering of unreasonable or unnecessary barriers to adoption of smart grid technologies, practices, and services.

Time-of-day pricing, determined in such a way as to minimize congestion on the grid and to maximize generation efficiency, will allow customers to make informed decisions about how to lower their electricity costs.

Demand-response control can assist utilities when unexpected supply losses occur or during periods of unprecedented demand. Utilities, regional transmission authorities, and independent system operators contract with customers who can support power losses in their operations in exchange for compensation. If a system operator encounters an unexpected need for reserve power, they may temporarily disconnect these contracted customers to restore reserve availability until demand falls or additional generation comes online. Demand response capability is critical to creating a more resilient power delivery system, one of the major goals of the smart grid. This communication between utility and consumer already exists for a subset of customers, but the communication may soon become more pervasive and subtle as new technologies are integrated into the system and device-to-device or device-to-subsystem communications become standardized.

Smart Metering and Variable Pricing

A significant component of the future smart grid is composed of changes within homes and businesses that will provide customers with awareness of their real-time power consumption as well as the ability to control that demand. Time-of-day pricing, determined in such a way as to minimize congestion on the grid and to maximize generation efficiency, will allow customers to make informed decisions about how to lower their electricity costs, even if the total amount of energy used over the course of a day remains the same.

One such innovation that should affect the grid's operation is the introduction of smart electricity meters, which differ from regular meters by providing real-time two-way communication between the meter and the utility. This not only provides the utility real-time awareness of every customer's usage, but also allows the utility to share the information with that customer through online tools. This information can be aggregated to provide various metrics to the customer, giving them the opportunity to set goals to reduce their consumption. These goals can be attained more easily with the introduction of smart appliances. These appliances have Internet connectivity, allowing them to share usage data with the utility, and through the same online tool, the customer. This gives customers the ability to observe not only how much power they use in real time but the specific devices in their home that are using that electricity.

Smart appliances may also mean utilities can use them as additional tools in their demand-response arsenal, allowing them to be remotely shut off during peak demand, reducing costs for the utility and the customer. Smart meters can also enable real-time pricing, which means customers pay a price more representative of the actual cost of generating the electricity they use. Real-time pricing provides a market signal to customers to reduce their use during peak demand, which is the most expensive time of day for the utility and also the most polluting, as it often involves the use of peaking generators, which can respond to rapid demand changes at the expense of efficiency and emissions. . . .

Electrical energy storage will need to be very cheap and very efficient in order to provide a compelling value proposition . . .

Storing Energy for Use During Peak Hours

One of the most interesting and complicated aspects of grid-scale energy storage is that there are many applications that create value on the grid. It is difficult to fully anticipate exactly what opportunities for arbitrage will develop as more communication among devices, consumers, producers, and distributers of electricity become develop. A report by the New York State Energy Research and Development Authority (NYSERDA) covers the range of possible methods to create value with grid-scale energy storage [for sale and use during peak hours or on demand]. These applications include power-oriented (high rate, short duration) and energy-oriented (longer duration) options for operators, end-users, and renewable power.

It is an interesting challenge for storage, both in terms of the technology requirements for the energy storage systems, as well as how to treat it. Electrical energy storage will need to be very cheap and very efficient in order to provide a compelling value proposition, but some of the system-level requirements for portable power and for automotive applications can be relaxed. It is worth noting that if storage only exists at the customer location to reduce demand during peak times, it can provide some value, but such implementations will not handle the challenge of putting stored energy back onto the grid. A simple form of storage is thermal energy storage, particularly attractive in warmer climates, where electricity, which is generally cheap in the middle of the night, is used to produce ice, which can then be stored and used to offset air conditioning demand during the daytime. This type of storage doesn't allow for utilities, generators, or customers to put energy back on the grid during peak demand times, but it does mitigate the demand on the system during the hottest, and often most energy-intensive, parts of the day. . . .

Reductions in effective peak demand will mean fewer expensive power plants will have to be dispatched, reducing the cost of peak power and minimizing customer incentive to change behavior. While this use of storage may reduce customer interest in reducing their peak use, utilities operational goal of more stable demand would still be achieved. This may appear a far more expensive way to reduce variations in demand, however, if placed appropriately within the T&D [transmission and distribution] system, using storage for arbitrage [making a profit off price fluctuations between peak and non-peak hours] also ensures that all renewable energy generated will eventually be dispatched. Even so, grid storage units have yet to achieve economies of scale, and so the capital costs of storage facilities might be hard to justify. Technologists who work on developing batteries for these applications will have to pay special attention to capital and operating costs, as well as to round-trip efficiency and battery lifetimes. . . .

2

A Smart Energy Grid Will Gradually Impact Energy Production

Lawrence J. Makovich

Lawrence J. Makovich is the vice president and senior advisor of the Global Power Group at IHS Cambridge Energy Research Associates, a company that helps energy-related businesses plan for the uncertain future of energy markets.

The vision of a smart energy grid replacing an antiquated system heavily dependent on fossil-fuel-burning power plants is often overly optimistic. There are no small-scale power supply centers in place, and the notion of real-time pricing for energy has yet to penetrate the residential sector in any meaningful way. In fact, the belief that smart meters in homes will decrease energy use and lower prices for users is rather unrealistic. Other forces are driving energy prices up so that the "smart use" of energy cannot yet offset consumer costs. It is, therefore, a mistake to think that a smart grid will revolutionize the energy system in short order. The energy supply and delivery system in the United States is constantly evolving to take advantage of new technologies, and change will progress gradually, as it always has.

There is a widespread expectation in the United States and around the world today that the smart grid is the next big thing, a disruptive technology poised to transform the electric power sector. The belief is that the use of smart meters and

Lawrence J. Makovich, "The Smart Grid: Separating Perception from Reality," *Issues in Science & Technology*, vol. 27, no. 3, Spring 2011.

other devices and systems will allow consumers to manage their own electricity use to radically reduce energy costs. The implementation of a smart grid system will enable the widespread use of renewable energy sources, allow more-distributed electricity generation, and help reduce carbon emissions.

The reality, however, is more complex and sobering. The smart grid idea is more accurately characterized as an extension of innovations that have been ongoing for decades. Change will continue but will be incremental because the technology is still evolving and because most consumers do not want the more flexible and uncertain pricing schemes that would replace the predictable and stable pricing of today's system. Indeed, it appears that most consumers, at least in the short term, will not benefit from moving to a smart grid system. Although a smart grid would probably help slow increases in electricity bills in the long run, it will not reduce them, because too many other factors will be pushing prices and power usage up in the years ahead.

Smart Grid Is Off to a Slow Start

The evidence from an IHS Cambridge Energy Research Associates study, which draws on the knowledge and experience of those closest to smart grid implementation, is that the smart grid "revolution" is off to a bumpy start and that there will be many more bumps in the road ahead. That road is still worth pursuing, but we will need to develop a more realistic understanding of how the electric power system in the United States is evolving. Instead of a demand-side-driven transformation of consumer behavior and the elimination of future capacity needs, expect a supply-side, engineering-driven application of smart grid technologies to improve network operation and reliability in the short term and to slow growth in generating capacity needs in the long run. In many respects, we already have a smart grid in the United States. In coming decades, we will be moving to a "smarter" grid. The pace will be gradual, but the eventual benefits will be real.

The Optimistic Smart Grid Vision

In the United States and other developed countries, an appealing and optimistic vision of the future smart grid has gained credence, even though the move toward a smarter grid is likely to turn out quite differently. In the current narrative, the United States and others are currently crippled by a balkanized "dumb" grid with endemic cascading failures, a result of continued reliance on antiquated, century-old technology. The solution is the smart grid: a continental-scale network of power lines incorporating advanced meters, sensing, and communication and control technologies that are linked through universal standards and protocols. It will be coordinated with advanced two-way broadband communication technologies that feed data into complex optimization software systems, allowing control technologies to deliver a more secure, self-healing, higher-quality, and lower-cost power network.

In many respects, we already have a smart grid in the United States. In coming decades, we will be moving to a "smarter" grid. The pace will be gradual, but the eventual benefits will be real.

Smart grid deployment, the story continues, will dramatically reshape power use. The smart grid will present consumers with real-time power prices and displays of information regarding power use by specific end uses. These price signals and information streams will empower consumers to have more control over their power consumption. Consequently, the smart grid will alter consumer decisions either directly through behavioral changes or indirectly through preprogrammed smart appliances and control applications. As a result, market failures will be fixed and much of the low-hanging fruit of the efficiency gap will be harvested. These efficiency gains will provide enough savings to drive monthly power bills lower. In addition, the gains in reducing peak power demand will be more than enough to offset the baseline growth in power in the future. Consequently, the smart grid will eliminate the need to build conventional power plants in the years ahead.

The smart grid will also enable a transformation in power supply, the narrative says. Indeed, eventually the smart grid will allow renewable sources such as wind and solar to supplant traditional sources. The use of small-scale, distributed-generation resources will lead to a significant decarbonization of future power production. "Smart systems may well be mankind's best hope for dealing with pressing environmental problems, notably global warming," said the *Economist* in a November 6, 2010, special report.

The smart grid narrative also envisions a rapid increase in electric vehicles, which will generate power or act as batteries in the grid. In time, there will no longer be a need to build conventional power plants to deal with peak power periods because of the new distributed, small-scale power generation.

Finally, according to the current narrative, the pace of smart grid investment, including widespread installation of smart meters, demonstrates that smart grid technology is reliable, economical, and gaining enough momentum that the smart grid will be ubiquitous in power systems within a decade.

The above story about the smart grid has been repeated so often by industry leaders, technologists, and the media that is has taken on a life of its own. It is appealing because it reflects optimism that a disruptive technology can transform the power sector by solving problems that otherwise appear difficult and expensive to address with current technology, and that it can do so without downsides. But this vision is also too good to be true. In reality, forcing a technological transformation of the power sector through the deployment of smart grid technologies along with real-time power prices appears to be not only a formidable task but also not a very likely outcome any time soon.

The Reality of Real-Time Pricing

Dynamic or real-time pricing, the ability to price electricity based on moment-to-moment changes in production costs, is expected to be the killer app of an emerging smart grid. The reality is that although some consumers can benefit from smart grid capabilities and dynamic pricing schemes, the majority cannot.

Real-time pricing is not a new idea. Economists have long considered the ability to use real-time prices that reflect the marginal cost of electricity at different times of the day as a more economically efficient way to price electricity. The Public Utility Regulatory Policy Act of 1978 encouraged utilities to use time-of-use-based rates to price electricity. Congress, in the Energy Policy Act of 2005, encouraged state regulators and utilities to shift from fixed rates to time-varied electric rates in order to increase energy efficiency and demand response.

[F]orcing a technological transformation of the power sector through the deployment of smart grid technologies along with real-time power prices appears to be not only a formidable task but also not a very likely outcome any time soon.

But most consumers focus on their pocketbook rather than the theoretical basis of this supposedly more efficient pricing system. After all, the prospect of real-time pricing involves higher and more unpredictable prices; on an hour-to-hour basis, the marginal cost of electricity is hard to predict and can change by a factor of 100 during any given day. Research clearly indicates that most consumers far prefer the stable and predictable power pricing schemes they currently have.

Real-time power prices are usually higher than traditional rates during peak periods and lower during off-peak periods. But most consumers use more electricity during peak periods than during off-peak periods. Thus, unless they can shift enough of their power use, typical consumers face a higher bill with a move to real-time pricing. Most consumers, according to research, doubt they can do this and expect that real-time pricing will increase their bills. . . .

Currently, there are no real-time pricing mandates for small customers . . . anywhere in the United States.

Resistance to Real-Time Pricing

A majority of power customers are not clamoring for access to dynamic pricing. So what explains the enthusiasm expressed by many who have participated in smart grid pilot projects? First and foremost is the fact that the programs have been voluntary. As a result, participants are self-selected members of a small set of the population who are inclined to try a new technology because they like experimenting with innovations. But self-selection bias can make pilot-project results unreliable as an indicator of how the larger population is likely to react to the new technology. It is risky to assume that if other consumers were to learn about these programs or were required to participate, they would end up loving them too. Mandatory participation could also lead to a backlash and derail any significant implementation of the technology.

Indeed, a bit of a backlash has already occurred. Many smart grid initiatives are going forward without any dynamic pricing schemes and those that do use dynamic prices employ highly muted price signals. Currently, there are no real-time pricing mandates for small customers (residential or small commercial) anywhere in the United States. This outcome of the regulatory process aligns with lessons from the past. The Maine Public Utility Commission mandated time-of-use rates for large-use residential consumers during the late 1980s, and the state of Washington mandated such rates for 300,000 residential consumers served by Puget Sound Energy in 2001. But in both cases most consumers were not able to shift enough usage to lower their electric bills, and the programs were eliminated within two years. In addition, these consumer preferences often translate into laws and regulations. California passed a law prohibiting dynamic pricing for residential customers, and New York imposed restrictions on the use of such pricing.

Many states, however, have recognized that some residential customers have the flexibility in power use to benefit from dynamic pricing and have required utilities to install a smart meter at the customer's request. As expected, only a minority of consumers have requested the meters. Also as expected, these consumers are primarily large industrial firms. However, even for larger consumers, the offerings typically involve dampened price signals that fall far short of real dynamic pricing.

Supply-Side Missteps

In addition to lackluster consumer demand, there have also been bumps on the supply side, as utilities have struggled to install the equipment and systems needed to make the smart grid work. There have been notable examples of technology problems and cost overruns, indicating that smart grid technologies and their optimal technical configurations are not yet proven and fully commercially available.

[T]he direct benefits of smart grid investments have not yet proven certain or significant enough to fully offset the costs of implementation.

- In Boulder, Colorado, Xcel Energy's costs to implement a smart grid program have soared from an estimated $15.2 million in 2008 to $42.1 million in February 2010.

- In Texas, Oncor Electric Delivery Company installed smart meters that later turned out not to comply with the standards set by the Public Utilities Commission of Texas. Oncor was subsequently allowed to recover $686 million from customers to install meters incorporating the new standards, as well as recover the $93 million cost of obsolete smart meters that were never installed.
- In California, the communication system included in the original smart meter deployment at Pacific Gas and Electric Company (PG&E) turned out to be incompatible with the communication and control needs of the evolving smart grid applications. PG&E was allowed to increase prices to recover almost $1 billion of associated costs. In addition, in November of 2009, PG&E was forced to temporarily stop deploying smart meters in Bakersfield, California—part of its $2.2 billion, 10-million smart meter deployment program—because of consumer complaints and lawsuits concerning perceptions of billing errors. Although these perceptions turned out to be wrong, the backlash illustrates the problem of attempting to roll out the smart grid program at the same time that power prices were increasing. . . .

As the above examples make clear, the direct benefits of smart grid investments have not yet proven certain or significant enough to fully offset the costs of implementation. The implication is clear: The United States is not moving to a rapid full-scale deployment of smart grid technologies and systems anytime soon. Future implementation is likely to be phased in by customer segments and be geographically uneven and far from complete in one decade.

A More Realistic Outlook

A more realistic vision of the future begins with the recognition that the smart grid is an incremental technology trend well under way rather than a disruptive technology that will transform the power sector in the next decade. The evolution toward a smarter grid has been taking place for several decades, as the power sector has incorporated available and emerging monitoring, automation, and control and communications technologies into the grid in varying degrees. These developments have already produced tangible gains: reduced costs for metering and for service connections and disconnections, as well as improved detection and isolation of problems during power outages and faster restoration of power. These gains in security and reliability have thus far reinforced the traditional grid and large central station power system rather than created economic forces pushing toward a distributed supply structure. As a result of these changes, it is inaccurate to think of the U.S. system as having a dumb grid that technology is poised to transform into a smart grid. Instead, smart technologies are already adding another layer of visibility to the condition and operation of the grid and also adding another layer of reliability by enhancing the capabilities needed to predict potential instabilities in the system. In short, the evolution to a smarter grid is helping to maintain and improve the high levels of reliability to which consumers have become accustomed.

3

New Energy Transmission Lines May Not Increase Use of Renewable Energy

David Morris

David Morris is vice president of the Institute for Local Self-Reliance, an organization that works with citizens and policy-makers on designing environmentally sound projects on the local level. He is the author of three books on the history and future of the US electricity system, including Seeing the Light: Regaining Control of Our Electricity System.

One proposed solution to providing more energy to congested areas of the country is to invest in new high-voltage transmission lines to bring renewable power from remote locations to the places where it is needed. The federal government has already determined that the nation shall have high-voltage corridors to stretch the new lines. However, such a plan fails to consider the rights of the states that have to deal with the unsightliness and environmental impact of these lines, and it rejects alternative solutions at the local level that may render these power corridors as unnecessary. Above all, though, the plan to bring outside renewable energy into specific regions ignores the fact that renewable energy can be produced near congested areas as well as remote locations and that building these corridors may require so much investment capital that power prices would not go down. Building networks of costly transmission lines will not spur the growth of this important sector—the only real solution is to increase the number of renewable energy sources.

The new mantra in energy circles is "national smart grid."

In [a 2008 column for] the *New York Times*, [former US Vice President] Al Gore insists the new president should give the highest priority to "the planning and construction of a unified national smart grid." President Barack Obama, responding to a question by MSNBC's Rachel Maddow, declares that one of "the most important infrastructure projects that we need is a whole new electricity grid . . . a smart grid."

We lump together the two words, "national" and "smart" as if they were joined at the hip, but in fact each describes and enables a very different electricity future. The word "national" in these discussions refers to the construction of tens of thousands of miles of *new* national ultra-high-voltage transmission lines, an initiative that would further separate power plants from consumers, and those who make the electricity decisions from those who feel the impact of those decisions.

The word "smart," on the other hand, refers to upgrading the *existing* network to make it more resilient and efficient. A smart grid can decentralize both generation and authority. Sophisticated electronic sensors, wireless communication, software and ever-more powerful computers will connect electricity customers and suppliers in real time, making possible a future in which tens of millions of households and businesses actively interact with the electricity network as both consumers and producers.

Congestion reveals a problem; it doesn't demand a specific solution.

Faulty Arguments

Advocates of a new national ultra-high-voltage transmission network offer three main arguments:

1. *New high-voltage transmission lines are needed to decrease electric grid congestion and therefore increase reliability and security.*

There is indeed congestion on some parts of our distribution and transmission networks. Congestion reveals a problem; it doesn't demand a specific solution. It can be addressed by reducing demand through increasing energy efficiency or by increasing on-site or local energy production, strategies often less costly and quicker to implement than building new transmission lines. An analogy from the solid-waste sector may be appropriate. Exhausting nearby landfills does not inevitably require us to send our garbage to newly constructed and more distant landfills. We can emphasize recycling, composting, scrap-based manufacturing and reuse.

2. *A new national high-voltage transmission network is necessary to dramatically increase renewable energy.*

President Obama wants to build new transmission lines because, "I want to be able to get wind power from North Dakota to population centers, like Chicago." Writing in *Vanity Fair* [in May, 2008], Robert F. Kennedy Jr. wants a new high-voltage transmission system to "deliver solar, wind, geothermal and other renewable energy across the country."

But do we really need to deliver renewable energy across the country? The distinguishing characteristic of renewable energy is its availability in abundant quantities virtually everywhere.

High-voltage transmission lines are not necessary to dramatically expand renewable-energy generation.

The Institute for Local Self-Reliance recently pulled together the modest amount of data available on the amount of renewable energy available in each state. Our report, "Energy Self-Reliant States," concludes that at least half the 50 states could meet all of their internal electricity demand with renewable energy found inside their borders, and all states could meet their current renewable electricity mandates from home-grown energy sources.

High-voltage transmission lines are not necessary to dramatically expand renewable-energy generation. But they are essential if we want to expand coal-generated electricity, because coal is found in limited places, and coal-fired power plants tend to be very large and therefore must serve very large markets. This is why, until recently, the primary advocates for new high-voltage transmission lines were those who wanted to construct large coal-fired power plants.

One of the most effective ways to stop new coal-fired power plants is to stop building new high-voltage transmission lines.

Before building new transmission lines, we should first investigate how much capacity there is on existing lines. Tellingly, that data is not readily available. A several-year campaign in Minnesota by the North American Water Office led to the nation's first utility-led analysis of the capacity on the existing transmission system in one part of the state. The results were so positive the state legislature ordered the utilities to expand the analysis.

The most recent study's data suggest that Minnesota can achieve its renewable electricity mandate of 25 percent by 2020 without building any major new networks of high-voltage transmission lines . . . .

3. *New transmission lines allow us to harness renewable energy in its best locations, thereby lowering costs.*

Many would argue that although renewable energy is available virtually everywhere, sunshine is more plentiful and the winds are stronger in a few locations, and therefore by generating electricity in those locations, we save money. Sunny Nevada, for example, can produce solar electricity from solar panels for about 20 percent less than Iowa and about 35 percent less than in Pittsburgh. A wind turbine in windy North

Dakota could produce electricity at a cost close to 30 percent lower than the same turbine located in Ohio.

But in most cases, these significant variations in production costs result in modest variations in the final cost of energy to the ultimate consumer, because more remote generation resources have an added cost of transporting the energy across long distances. For example, my colleague John Farrell estimates that if Ohio's electricity came from North Dakota wind farms—1,000 miles away—the cost of constructing new transmission lines to carry that power, and the electricity losses suffered during transmission, could surpass the lower cost of production.

Even if modest financial savings do occur, they are easily outweighed by the arduous and contentious prospect of having to seize or negotiate for the use of the land of hundreds of thousands of farmers, homeowners and businesses to build the new lines.

Some advocates estimate the full cost of a new national transmission grid at $100 billion.

Rethinking the Arguments for More Transmission Lines

The arguments against building and overlaying a new national transmission system are more compelling:

1. *Building a new high-voltage transmission line diverts resources from the more important task of making the best use of the existing electrical network and integrating the new generation of decentralizing energy technologies.*

Some advocates estimate the full cost of a new national transmission grid at $100 billion. In these tough credit markets, as states and the federal government design financial incentives that make it easier and more financially attractive to build high-voltage transmission lines, they undermine the potential for energy efficiency and decentralized production. Richard Cowart, director of the Regulatory Assistant Project noted back in 2002, "Over-investing in transmission will tend to support remote generation and undermine the value of distributed resources. Under-investing in transmission will have the opposite effect."

2. *Building new transmission lines requires the federal government to increasingly pre-empt state and local authority, which may undermine a generation of advances in state electricity regulation.*

To accelerate the construction of ultra-high-voltage transmission lines, the federal government may well have to pre-empt state and local authority, because states and localities and their citizenry will not look kindly on tens of thousands of miles of new transmission lines crossing their lands to deliver power to distant communities. Indeed, it is the fear of popular opposition to such transmission lines that fuels the drive for pre-emption.

Billionaire T. Boone Pickens, the country's most visible proponent of a national transmission system, bluntly told Congress a few months ago that he is "disconcerted that state public authorities . . . are required to consider the benefits of the project to the citizens of their state." He worries that, "Where state utility commissions are limited by state law to considering benefits to citizens of their state, eminent-domain power may not be available to transmission developers wishing to cross the state without providing transmission service to local generators or local electricity users." He wants Congress to give the Federal Energy Regulatory Commission "exclusive jurisdiction" to site new transmission lines.

An increasing centralization of authority over electricity planning has been slowly occurring over the last 15 years. It was speeded up with the passage of the 2005 Energy Act that requires the Department of Energy to designate "national interest electric transmission corridors." Once designated, state regulatory bodies have one year to approve an application for a new transmission line, or the federal government can step in and issue the approval.

[S]tates complained that in designating transmission corridors, the DOE had refused to consider non-transmission solutions to congestion problems . . .

Other Solutions Should Be Considered

It is instructive to see how the federal government has exercised this newly acquired authority to designate national interest transmission corridors. In late 2007, DOE [Department of Energy] released its first group of designated transmission corridors, setting off an immediate outcry by the affected states. Governments and regulatory agencies in Pennsylvania, Virginia, Delaware, Maryland and New Jersey all petitioned for a rehearing. DOE rejected their petition.

Over the last 30 years, grassroots activism has pushed state energy regulatory agencies away from their traditional focus on encouraging bigger power plants and higher-voltage transmission lines and toward a new decision-making matrix called "least cost planning." Utilities are required to examine and pursue alternatives like increasing energy efficiency or installing smaller, dispersed power plants before they can build new traditional power plants or transmission lines. Recently, states also require utilities to take into account environmental costs and to give renewable energy a priority.

The states complained that in designating transmission corridors, the DOE had refused to consider non-transmission solutions to congestion problems, something their own state laws require, as does the Federal Power Act. The FPA specifically directs the DOE to issue its report only "after considering alternatives."

The New Jersey Board of Public Utilities asked the DOE to refrain from designating corridors "until after it analyzed whether alternative means, including energy efficiency, demand response and clean local generation within the critical congestion area could relieve congestion more effectively, at lower cost, with less harm to the environment, with better assurance of the reliability and security of our electricity supply, or with less vulnerability to uncertainties such as future fuel costs, future environmental requirements and other variables."

The DOE claimed that an examination of non-transmission solutions was outside its jurisdiction. According to the DOE's perverse interpretation of the law, the federal government can pre-empt state authority but it cannot take into account the same factors states do in deciding whether to approve new transmission lines, even though almost everyone agrees that consideration of those factors results in better decisions.

The Mid-Atlantic Area National Interest Electric Transmission Corridor that the DOE designated encompasses nearly all the state of Maryland and New Jersey. New Jersey complained, arguing that the DOE's own data indicated that much of these areas are not experiencing transmission constraints or congestion. The DOE did not deny New Jersey's allegation but maintained, "(T)he statute does not appear to foreclose the possibility of national corridor designation in the absence of current congestion . . . even without congestion, DOE can approve a line where it wants to encourage 'desirable generation.'"

It is unclear where President Obama stands on the growing state-federal controversy.

In this case, the DOE decided that coal-fired power plants constituted desirable generation. The uncongested parts of the DOE's designated corridor were largely in areas of Ohio, Pennsylvania, Virginia and West Virginia that account for more than two-thirds of the coal produced in the Appalachian region.

Hesitation and Indecision at the Federal Level

This is the context for Obama's presidency. It is unclear whether he will emphasize "national" or "smart." Obama's fiscal stimulus plan calls for $11 billion for what he calls a smart grid investment program. The program specifically mentions spending on new high-voltage transmission lines, but it also encompasses investments in smart grids. Since the federal government has direct control over high-voltage transmission lines through the Federal Energy Regulatory Commission but not over the retail subtransmission and distribution networks, it might find it easier to push money toward the former ("national") rather than the latter ("smart").

The DOE's decisions to date on national interest transmission corridors have come while George W. Bush was president. It is unclear where President Obama stands on the growing state-federal controversy. At his confirmation hearing, Secretary of Energy-designate Steven Chu declared a nationwide grid "in the national interest" and insisted the country needed a "new way of doing business" to get it built quickly.

However, when Sen. Robert Mendendez, D-N.J., protested about the DOE's process in declaring most of New Jersey a federal pre-emption corridor, Chu acknowledged the problem and ended up saying that new lines must be sited "in a way that takes into consideration the local feelings but yet also recognizes the national needs."

Will Chu require the DOE, and will President Obama ask FERC [the Federal Energy Regulatory Commission], to evaluate petitions for new transmission lines using the same least-cost-planning process now used by many states?

Will the federal government require all utilities to undertake the same analysis done in Minnesota to identify the capacity of existing transmission lines to absorb more renewable energy?

Will fiscal stimulus spending on upgrading the electricity grid emphasize smart over national?

The shape of our electricity future might depend on the answers to these questions.

4

The US Electric Grid Should Be Underground

Patrick Maas

Patrick Maas is a veteran of the travel industry, holding jobs in travel distribution and global sales and finance. He runs a blog called Maas Media that posts musings on travel and politics.

Much of the US electrical transmission network is aboveground, creating eyesores and leading to power outages when inclement weather brings down power lines. Wires buried underground are more attractive because they are less prone to failures in service, but the cost of converting aboveground lines to belowground networks is costly. Currently, the United States cannot bear the burden of increased taxes and energy rates needed to recoup the costs of making the transition. However, when the economy improves, the nation should consider the advantages of running all power lines underground.

Have you ever wondered why the power seldom goes out in Manhattan, New York City? It's because the power-grid, including phone/internet, gas and cable is buried underground!

I used to live in Oakland Park, Florida and it pretty much guaranteed that my power would go out every time a summer thunder-storm would roll through the area. I can't count the number of times I sat without power; sometimes even for days during hurricane season. For those people who've never

Patrick Maas, "Should the U.S. Electric Grid Be Underground," Maas Media-Travel & Political Musings, February 4, 2011. www.patrickmaas.com.

lived in the south, it sucks to be without A/C [air conditioning] in July or August. My friends living further out west in Weston, Florida never had these types of issues. Why? You guessed it, their power-grid was completely buried underground.

So why with all the hurricanes that strike the Gulf Region, all the Tornadoes that strike the Midwest and all the ice/snow storms that strike the Northeast aren't we burying all utilities underground?

Comparing the Advantages and Disadvantages of Buried Lines

Very simple, it costs a lot of money to change the existing above ground system to an underground system. Yet, many regions across the country are slowly adapting to underground services, especially in new construction communities and in heavily congested areas such as downtown areas of larger cities. So let's take a look at the disadvantages versus advantages of underground utilities with the emphasis on the electric grid to keep it simple for argument sake.

Advantages for Underground Utilities

1. Eye-sore is gone. Let's face it; nobody wants to look outside their window and look at an ugly utility pole with wires hanging across your backyard or front-yard.

2. Power is more likely to stay on during weather related events such as wind, ice and snow. Trees won't fall on power-lines and ice/snow can't form on the lines, thus keeping your power on; even during a hurricane.

3. Safer—for the environment and people. No more need for cutting down trees for the thousands of utility poles that are needed to replace broken ones and people don't have to worry about the electromagnetic fields surrounding electric cables.

Disadvantages of Underground Utilities

1. Cost of Repairs—if something does go wrong with the underground cables then the cost is much higher versus above ground and it takes longer to fix.
2. Doesn't work well in flood prone area—it's a fact that if an area regularly floods during rain storms or flooding due to excessive snow melt, etc. the underground system tends to break down a lot more.

From the above it would seem that it would make sense to bury everything underground. If your power goes out 4–6 times per year (average for above ground utility) and then compare it against it only going out once every 2 years (average for underground utility) then most people would prefer an underground utility in their neighborhood; even if it meant that if the power goes out it may take a few extra hours to get the power back on.

Let's face it; nobody wants to look outside their window and look at an ugly utility pole with wires hanging across your backyard or front-yard.

The Cost of Converting to Buried Lines

It makes financial sense to bury everything underground when constructing a new community. The cost per household on average goes up by $500 for new construction. So a $175,000 home construction would cost an extra $500 to construct in order to have underground utilities or add about 0.3% to the cost. Needless to say, this makes sense. Not only for the city and the citizens, but for the utility company as well since it reduces maintenance costs over the long run.

The problem arises when cities want to switch from existing above ground utilities to underground utilities. The rough cost is about $1 million per mile to bury it underground. To give you an idea, FPL (Florida Power & Light) has a total of 64,000 miles of distribution lines. A little over a third, 24,000, is buried underground. Therefore, if FPL had to bury everything underground they would look at a total cost of 40,000 x $1 million = $40 billion! That's roughly $15k per customer or $9.5k if you want to split the cost amongst all customers, which needless to say is a huge amount of money. Even if you divested the cost over ten years for the consumer it would still add $79–$125/month to their electric bill. Not many customers will opt for that, I can guarantee you that . . .

It makes financial sense to bury everything underground when constructing a new community.

One may argue that if you take into consideration the cost annually associated with repairs to the system that it should pay for itself over an extended period of time, but that's not really the case. Case studies in North Carolina, Florida and Seattle have shown that it would only cover 15% in a worst case scenario and up to 38% in a best case scenario. So in Florida's case it would only save FPL about $15 billion, thus leaving them with a $25 billion gap.

The American Economy Cannot Support the Change

Most of Western Europe and most of Japan has gone underground in the past few decades, so why them and not the U.S.A.? The reason is that most countries in Europe heavily subsidized the construction of the underground utilities during the 70s and 80s and in today's political and financial climate there isn't going to be an appetite in the U.S. to spend tens of billions of dollars every year for this massive undertaking.

Going back to the FPL example; hypothetically for a 15 year project, FPL could cover the $15 billion in cost as that's the amount of money it's going to save in repairs/maintenance anyway, so in essence it doesn't cost them a dime. In other words the $1 billion per year they would spent on construction is earned back in a reduction of repairs. However, somebody will still need to cover the difference, which is $25 billion.

If you were to cut it in 3 parts then the Federal government would subsidize about $8.5 billion of it. The State would contribute another $8.5 billion and the consumer would have to cover the remaining $8 billion; again, all this spread out over 15 years so about $530–$565 million per year. This adds up to about $126 per FPL customer per year or about $10.50 per month extra in the electric bill.

Most of Western Europe and most of Japan has gone underground in the past few decades, so why them and not the U.S.A.?

Bear in mind that the State would have to come up with half a billion dollars per year as well, so it's likely they would need to raise revenues through the form of added utility taxes, unless of course they can find the money by cutting spending.

For now, it's more likely that municipalities will continue to force utilities and contractors to bury utilities underground for new construction projects, but existing above ground utilities are going to stay until a better financial/economical climate starts taking hold. Even then it's going to be an uphill battle for proponents to get this approved, but maybe another catastrophe will push the public and political appetite in that direction. Also, bear in mind the number of outages, including massive blackouts, has been going up by 9.5% per year since the early 1990s. The main reason for this is that the U.S. power grid is outdated. It was built over half a century ago, so maybe it may not be a bad idea to upgrade the system and bury the cables underground while we're at it . . .

5

The US Electric Grid Should Mirror the US Interstate System in Scope

Edward Krapels and Stephen Conant

Edward Krapels is the founder of Anbaric Holding, a private company that designs unique "smart grid" energy transmission solutions. Stephen Conant is the vice president of New England Transmission Projects for Anbaric Holding.

Given increasing demands for energy and the need to tap renewable and low-emission energy sources, the United States needs to adopt an interstate extra-high-voltage transmission system that will span and service all parts of the country. Although energy interests have begun planning for this system, few investors have committed to it because of its slow rate of financial return and the large outlays necessary to get such a project off the ground. In addition, state and local authorities have stymied these programs due to regulations and other hurdles. America cannot afford to take on these stumbling blocks piecemeal; rather, the country as a whole must approve the need for and build this new energy highway in the same way it approved and built the US transportation highway system.

A century ago, the transmission system reflected local needs. Fifty years ago, regional requirements began to be taken into account. Today national goals have taken priority. However, the grid is inadequate to achieve these goals.

Edward Krapels and Stephen Conant, "US Grid: It's Our Way or the Highway," *Power Engineering International*, November 1, 2008. www.powerengineeringint.com.

In the next 20 years, the US will need to make an intensive effort to expand its electrical transmission system. People are beginning to recognise that the expansion of the system is an essential component of any solution to several big problems that the US faces.

Energy Priorities

Today's first priority, as always, is grid reliability. The northeast blackout of 2003 brought this priority home and provided an opportunity to highlight years of underinvestment in the grid.

> *If the US is to accomplish its new energy missions . . . the country needs to develop a true nationwide, power grid version of its interstate highway system.*

The second priority is to address climate change and reduce the US's environmental footprint. The third is to contain the US's growing dependence on natural gas and avoid increasing the country's reliance on imported liquefied natural gas. The development of an interstate extra-high-voltage transmission system (EHV), through the adoption of a nationwide EHV strategy, can make a modern transmission grid the backbone of a strategy to address these important national issues.

Adopting such a strategy will mark an important shift in US energy policy. Sound energy policy requires a periodic assessment of the needs of consumers and of society as a whole. If the US is to accomplish its new energy missions—to combat climate change, while containing dependence on insecure imported natural gas—the country needs to develop a true nationwide, power grid version of its interstate highway system.

Over the past two decades, attention has been focused on developing competitive wholesale energy markets. Electricity market rules and regulations, however, have had the unintended consequence of discouraging diverse generating portfolios.

Under rules aimed at providing competition in the wholesale power markets, most investors would rather build plants and recoup their investment in just a few years than build facilities that take decades to recoup their investment costs. In other words, the US's preoccupation with developing competitive power markets within confined regions has not created a fertile climate for long-range, strategic investments in the projects that are needed to achieve today's major policy goals.

These projects include large wind farms, baseload clean coal and nuclear plants, and large EHV transmission projects. Of these, EHV transmission is unique in terms of the benefits it brings to the system. It provides the functional equivalent of an interstate highway system, allowing more efficient energy transport.

While on a highway system we talk about savings in terms of time and petrol consumption, on an interstate electrical transmission system we talk of the need for infrastructure, line loss and CO_2 [carbon dioxide] emission reductions.

Tapping Low-Emission Resources

From the broadest policy perspective, demand reduction and increased energy efficiency is the low-hanging fruit for reducing carbon emissions, but their potential is limited. With aggressive conservation measures, nationwide annual demand growth of one to two per cent may be slowed, but not eliminated. Inevitably new low-carbon supply side resources will be needed.

With nearly all hydroelectric resource in the US developed, there are just three large purely domestic sources for low-carbon electricity generation: renewables, including wind, geothermal, solar and biomass resources; nuclear power; and clean coal technologies with carbon storage and sequestration.

All three have received a great deal of public attention and policy support, as well as government incentives. A nuclear renaissance may yet be on the horizon in the US, and the inherent desirability of using coal (an abundant domestic fuel that now provides the country with 50 per cent of its electricity) in a less environmentally damaging way is extremely appealing. However, neither has received the overwhelming public support or private investment that the renewables industry has seen.

Renewables often have a problem, however. They are often remotely located, so an expansion of the transmission grid is needed to bring their energy to urban markets. For that to happen, a substantial expansion of the US EHV transmission system will be needed. If done properly, the expansion will support other supply resources that will also help achieve US reliability and fuel diversity goals.

The Energy Industry Is Already Looking Toward the Future

The careful coordination of national EHV expansion is essential. And that means adequate planning that should extend beyond state and regional boundaries. Questions regarding the appropriate level of transmission infrastructure are typically raised early in the planning process.

Renewables often have a problem, however. They are often remotely located, so an expansion of the transmission grid is needed to bring their energy to urban markets.

One of the challenges associated with regional planning is the scope of the solution sought. For many, the most desirable approach to transmission upgrades in a minimalist one, to minimize investment. According to this rationale, a transmission solution only need be as strong as the expectations placed on it.

Expectations, however, are growing. In the past few years, the need for the US to take action to reduce its carbon emissions has increasingly been accepted by a growing number of cities and states, and integrated into their energy and environmental planning.

Many cities have announced 'green' and renewables programmes. Renewable portfolio standards (RPS) have been adopted in a majority of US states and are a major driver in accelerating the development of renewable resources, especially wind.

According to a joint study involving the American Wind Energy Association (AWEA), the US Department of Energy and the National Renewable Energy Laboratory, wind could provide up to 20 per cent, or approximately 350 GW, of the nation's electricity. A 2008 update of that study concluded that "a 20 per cent wind scenario in 2030, while ambitious, could be feasible if the significant challenges identified in this report are overcome".

Further analysis by AWEA and the Association of Electricity Producers indicates that the system could "enable significantly greater wind energy penetration levels by providing an additional 200 to 400 GW [gigawatt] of bulk transmission capacity. The total capital investment is estimated at approximately $60 billion. While it is by no means the total solution, this initiative illustrates the opportunities that exist, and what might be possible with adequate cooperation, collaboration and coordination—the '3Cs'."

Planning, however, is not a solution in and of itself. Ultimately projects need to get built . . .

The development of these facilities under a 3Cs model requires planners to look beyond the traditional utility or regional transmission organization (RTO) boundaries toward interregional and international solutions.

Recently the Southwest Power Pool, the Midwest Independent System Operator, the PJM Regional Transmission Organization, Tennessee Valley Authority and the Department of Energy announced that they would hold a stakeholder meeting to discuss the development of a coordinated system plan for their areas.

The result was the Joint Coordinated System Plan initiative. This development has the potential to allow the industry to take a giant leap forward in terms of how it designs the system and how it establishes expectations in terms of what the nation's grid can deliver.

In many parts of the US, however, conflicting state and independent system operator (ISO) regulations are currently impeding transmission development aimed at bringing renewables to market.

Bearing the Costs of New Transmission Networks

Planning, however, is not a solution in and of itself. Ultimately projects need to get built, which raises the sticky question of who pays. Participants in the electricity sector have long been embroiled in often bitter disputes about who pays for transmission.

The challenges associated with the allocation of the costs of such projects run the risk of discouraging the development of the right transmission solutions. Well-chosen projects have to emerge from a complex dialogue about the proper allocation of transmission costs between national, regional, state and local regulators.

More than a decade of power industry restructuring has seen important changes in federal and regional transmission cost allocation policy. This policy template, however, has gradually been overshadowed by its own deficiencies, as well as by increased concerns about climate change.

In its place, both state and federal regulators have been increasingly willing to accept that the costs of certain transmission projects should be socialized. This requires an acceptance of the premise that the real value of transmission is enabling and improving competitive markets for an array of generation resources, where the benefits outweigh the cost of specific transmission projects.

Given the desire of the US to increase the diversity of its fuel portfolio and ensure that it maximizes its transmission system's overall efficiency, the US needs to move away from a project-by-project approach to infrastructure development.

The Nation Needs to Agree That Change Is Necessary

Those who believe that transmission is an essential facilitator of climate change solutions now have a primary mission for the grid that extends far beyond the narrow analysis of the beneficiaries of a specific project. Given the remote locations of resources, it is necessary to extend the EHV grid well beyond its current footprint to integrate these resources as a large portion of the nation's electricity supply in order to meet an emerging national need to reduce carbon emissions.

In many parts of the US, however, conflicting state and independent system operator (ISO) regulations are currently impeding transmission development aimed at bringing renewables to market.

Development rules worked out with great difficulty over the past decade—designed primarily to maintain reliability and promote competitive wholesale markets—often hinder the development of EHV transmission for renewables. It is in the single-state ISOs, such as California and Texas, that we have seen the most progressive transmission development policies specifically aimed at bringing large quantities of renewables to market.

California provides an interesting example of how the schism between state and regional interests plays out, however. Behind the leadership of the California Public Utilities Commission, the California ISO pioneered the Federal Energy Regulatory Commission's (FERC's) recognition in April 2007 of a third category of transmission line known as a trunk line to access what FERC refers to as "locationally constrained resources", meaning renewable energy resources such as wind, geothermal and solar resources.

While not prohibiting the use of the line by non-renewable generators, in effect, FERC agreed to allow ratepayers to fund transmission lines that do not meet traditional reliability or economic tests to achieve a different policy goal of encouraging development of renewable resources.

Meanwhile, Southern California Edison's (SCE's) attempt to build the Palo Verde/Devers II to access 5000 MW [megawatt] of gas-fired generation in the transmission constrained area of western Arizona was thwarted by rejection of the proposed line by the Arizona Corporate Commission, reinforcing the difficulty of building transmission lines across state borders. This is in stark contrast to the rate-based in-state transmission line to access 5000 MW of wind energy in the Tehachapi Mountains that SCE will build as a result of the FERC order.

Given the schisms among state, regional and national approaches to transmission planning and construction, using an EVH transmission grid to address the national priorities of building a reliable grid, reducing the US's environmental footprint and expanding the use of indigenous low- and no-carbon-based fuel will only be possible with a concerted national effort.

If the US is to accomplish the US's new energy missions—to combat climate change, while containing dependence on insecure imported natural gas—the country needs a true nationwide, power grid version of its interstate highway system.

6

Security Concerns Must Be Addressed for the Smart Grid to Be Successful

Jude Clemente

Jude Clemente is an energy security analyst with the Homeland Security Department at San Diego State University. He is also a technical writer whose work has appeared in Oil & Gas Journal, Pipeline & Gas Journal, The Journal of Energy Security, Petroleum World, *and* Managing Power.

While the design of a national "smart grid" to control power use and delivery in the United States is desirable, the industry and the government must consider the security of the system against potential attack from terrorists or other enemies. Because the planned grid will implement linked communications and control systems, security measures must be in place to address the possibility of hacking aimed at disrupting the system. In addition, the physical infrastructure of the system—power plants and transmission lines—are also vulnerable targets that must be protected. Finally, satellite images and trade journals are public sources of information that could aid enemies in planning attacks and knocking out key aspects of the grid. The government must have a plan that takes into account that much of this sensitive information is readily available in publications and on the Internet. Without securing the new smart grid, the entire enterprise may become more of a liability than an asset.

Jude Clemente, "The Security Vulnerabilities of Smart Grid," *Journal of Energy Security*, June 2009. The Institute for the Analysis of Global Security.

There is widespread agreement among energy security analysts, utilities, and policy-makers that the next evolution of the US electricity grid depends upon the reduction of transmission congestion and bottlenecks. Proposals to modernize the country's increasingly fragile electricity system have largely revolved around the potential deployment of "Smart Grid." This integrated electric network will incorporate advanced digital functions into the nation's electrical infrastructure to enhance reliability, efficiency, flexibility, and security. The Electric Power Research Institute (EPRI) considers Smart Grid one of the four infrastructures necessary to meeting climate change goals. In fact, EPRI has been selected by the National Institute of Standards and Technology to be the facilitator of Smart Grid's roadmap.

Al-Qaida and other terrorist networks specifically target power grids because electricity has no substitute and virtually every other key infrastructure depends upon access to power. . . .

The current electricity system includes a series of independently operating regional grids that would greatly benefit from the optimization that comes with national interconnection. Smart Grid has strong support. President [Barack] Obama's 2009 economic stimulus package allocates $4.5 billion to modernize the nation's electricity system and put Smart Grid technologies on the fast track. The development of Smart Grid, however, takes the US into uncharted territory regarding the organization and operation of the transmission system. The transformation will require both quantitative and qualitative changes in the way electricity is moved around the country. The current state of knowledge is not sufficient to fully grasp the implications of Smart Grid. The analysis presented here focuses on a concept that will be central to Smart Grid: security of the system.

Preventing Sabotage to the Grid

With increased interconnection, security concerns arise. Indeed, *The Wall Street Journal* recently reported [in 2009] cyber spies from China, Russia, and other countries may have penetrated the US electrical grid and implanted software programs that could be used to disrupt the system. Thus far, the focus to better secure the grid has understandably focused on the existing network, but Smart Grid's unique infrastructure must now become the spotlight to secure the system. Going forward, the US Department of Energy (DOE) confirms the ability to resist attack—by identifying and responding to disruptions caused by sabotage—is one of Smart Grid's seven crucial functions.

Objective 3.1 of the US Department of Homeland Security's (DHS) Strategic Plan Fiscal Years 2008–2013 aims to "Protect and Strengthen the Resilience of the Nation's Critical Infrastructure and Key Resources." Al-Qaida and other terrorist networks specifically target power grids because electricity has no substitute and virtually every other key infrastructure depends upon access to power. In their 2005 book, *Messages to the World: The Statements of Osama Bin Laden*, [Bruce] Lawrence and [James] Howarth report the Al-Qaeda leader warns that Americans "will not come to their senses unless the attacks fall on their heads and . . . until the battle has moved inside America." The asymmetrical warfare paradigm which terrorists explicitly adhere to must be taken into account by each Homeland Security policy enacted. Security vulnerabilities exist on three main fronts—physical, cyber, and open-source information. Smart Grid must become a hardened target.

Exposure of Physical Infrastructure

Smart Grid will derive its electricity from a combination of renewable and conventional energy sources. Physically, fortifying Smart Grid's critical infrastructure is a new and daunting challenge because renewable energy facilities in particular spread out over vast distances. Wind is generally viewed as the most likely renewable incremental electricity source over the next several decades. The American Wind Energy Association reports utility-scale turbines for land-based wind installations come with rotor diameters ranging up to 300 feet. DOE indicates typical turbine spacing is five to ten rotor diameters apart, leading to well over a half mile between turbines. DOE concludes generating 20% of electricity with land-based wind installations would demand at least 20,000 square miles. By comparison, all US nuclear power plants, which produce roughly 20% of power, occupy only 115 square miles.

Smart Grid will require a "backbone" of extra-high-voltage transmission lines, which carry between 345 and 765 kilovolts (kV) of electricity. These power lines will increase the capacity, efficiency, and reliability of the grid. To the extent wind is the source of new generation, tens of thousands of miles of new transmission lines and their support structures will need to be built. Most potential sites for large-scale wind (and solar) farms are removed from population centers. As Dan Reicher, Director of Climate Change and Energy Initiatives at Google, has pointed out on *GreenBiz*, Smart Grid "is going to require literally thousands and thousands of miles of new transmission."

An extended (and exposed) transmission system is a major Homeland Security concern because it is a preferred terrorist target.

In his well-marketed wind energy plan, oil tycoon T. Boone Pickens calls for 100,000 wind turbines and 40,000 miles of new high-voltage (230kV) transmission lines to be built in the Great Plains Region. The physical exposure of this infrastructure could compromise system security, however, as the bulk of new lines will need to be overhead transmission. [Bracken]

Hendricks (2009) has suggested burying lines underground will improve Smart Grid's security. Unfortunately, burying power lines is generally not feasible, as it makes them more susceptible to weather damage and slows repair time. Further, a 2006 study by the Edison Electric Institute (EEI) indicated putting power lines underground would cost about $1 million a mile compared with $100,000 to install overhead lines. EEI's report, *Out of Sight, Out of Mind?*, estimated statewide initiatives to bury power lines could prompt electricity rate increases of 80 to 125%.

[T]he US power grid could become an easier target for hackers as more elements of it are connected to each other or to the internet.

There are at least four layers of physical security that must work to complement each other in Smart Grid: 1) environmental design 2) mechanical and electronic access control 3) intrusion detection and 4) video monitoring. EPRI and a number of US utilities are now discussing the possibility of monitoring transmission lines by satellite. Currently, this security measure is not practical because satellites with high-resolution imagery do not pass overhead often enough to pick up sabotage attempts, and those satellites passing more frequently lack the necessary imaging capability. An extended (and exposed) transmission system is a major Homeland Security concern because it is a preferred terrorist target. In the 2005 report, Diagnostic Tools to Estimate Consequences of Terrorism Attacks Against Critical Infrastructure, New York University's [Rae] Zimmerman et al. examined international databases, maintained by the National Memorial Institute for the Prevention of Terrorism, tracking terrorist attacks on the world's electricity sector from 1994–2004. . . . In terms of the total number of physical attacks, transmission systems are easily the most common target. . . .

Hacking into the Power Grid

Known as cyber-physical systems (CPS), [Go] Zonghua says the emergence of "physical and engineered systems whose operations are integrated, monitored, and controlled by a computational core" is creating new security complexities (Second International Workshop on Cyber-Physical Systems).

As opposed to embedded systems that typically use standalone devices, CPS infrastructure optimizes interacting components. The internet powers the man-machine interaction and their "smart" communication. Unfortunately, the US power grid could become an easier target for hackers as more elements of it are connected to each other or to the internet. Smart Grid utilizes intelligent electricity transmission-and-distribution networks that use two-way consumption data to make power delivery more efficient, reliable, and safe. The installation of advanced metering infrastructure solutions, such as smart meters, help consumers monitor energy usage in real-time by measuring, collecting, and analyzing data.

Smart Grid features are intended to enhance the security of the national electrical infrastructure, but the extension of two-way digital communications could make protecting the power grid from a cyber attack a far more complicated mission—extra nodes on a network can become new openings for intruders. IOActive, a computer security services firm, reports an attacker with $500 in equipment and a basic electrical background could seize command of Smart Grid's bilateral communication system to manipulate services to homes and businesses. Once the system has been penetrated, the saboteur could cause a blackout by: 1) gaining control of possibly millions of meters on the grid and simultaneously shutting them down or 2) disrupting the load balance of the local system by suddenly decreasing or increasing the demand for power.

In a recent brief to DHS, IOActive researchers announced they had "created a computer worm that could quickly spread among Smart Grid devices, many of which use wireless technology to communicate." Hackers could cut power to those Smart Grid devices that use "remote disconnect," a feature that allows utilities to stop power flow to customers. Industrial leaders articulated concerns to Congress earlier this year that a rush to establish Smart Grid without substantial security precautions could result in wasted resources if new technologies require replacement shortly after deployment. GridLAB-D and other power distribution simulation and analysis systems are using the most advanced modeling techniques to ensure that those technologies expected to play a long-term role are interoperable and secure.

Grid Technologies at Risk

DOE's National Energy Technology Laboratory groups Smart Grid technologies into five categories:

1. *Integrated Communications*—connect components to an open architecture for real-time information and control, to allow every part of the grid to both "talk" and "listen"

2. *Sensing and Measurement*—technologies support faster and more accurate response, such as remote monitoring, time-of-use pricing, and demand-side management

3. *Advanced Components*—apply the latest research in superconductivity, fault tolerance, storage, power electronics, and diagnostics

4. *Advanced Control Methods*—monitor essential components, enabling rapid diagnosis and precise solutions appropriate to any event

5. *Improved Interfaces and Decision Support*—amplify human decision-making, transforming grid operators and managers into knowledge workers

The deployment of these technologies should be a judicious process, as US success or failure, in all likelihood, determines the probability other nations will upgrade their own electrical infrastructure. "The more you push communications, intelligence [across the grid] . . . you are adding some level of risk," Brian Seal, a senior project manager involved in power delivery at EPRI, recently told the Associated Press. William Sanders, principal investigator for the National Science Foundation Cyber Trust Center, says, "I do not think we should stop deployment until we have it all worked out. But we have to be vigilant and address security issues in Smart Grid early on." The North American Electric Reliability Corporation has created a number of cyber security standards, but recent Senate legislation, namely the Critical Electric Infrastructure Protection Act, makes it clear federal leadership needs consolidated. The authority of DHS and the Federal Energy Regulatory Commission (FERC) to secure the electric grid is expected to increase.

Public sources, terrorism experts conclude, can be used to gain at least 80% of the information required to plot an attack on Smart Grid.

Too Much Sensitive Information Is Available to the Public

In the ever-expanding world of open-source information, Smart Grid's greatest strength could also be its greatest weakness: modern technology. The growing ability of terrorists to readily collect intelligence and identify infrastructural weak spots makes electrical grids more susceptible to sabotage. For example, according to the US Department of Defense (DoD), a captured Al-Qaida training manual claims, "Using public sources openly and without resorting to illegal means, it is possible to gather at least 80% of information about the enemy." Public sources, terrorism experts conclude, can be used to gain at least 80% of the information required to plot an attack on Smart Grid. When it comes to targeting the US electrical grid, however, it could be possible to collect all the information needed, as publicly available trade journals disclose where new electrical facilities are being constructed. These journals document the transmission capacity of switching stations and the geographic areas for which they are responsible.

Terrorists have long realized disrupting the US information infrastructure is a far less risky strategy than traditional military combat. The internet, for example, gives terrorists a readily available, mostly unguarded corridor where they can hide their location, select their entryway, and mask their identity. Indeed, a recent intelligence report by the US Army confirmed popular micro-blogging services, such as Twitter and MySpace, Global Positioning System maps, and voice-changing software are all possible terrorist tools. The internet is an ideal arena for fundraising, recruitment, and data mining. The US Institute of Peace points out the variety of reasons terrorist networks use the internet to gather intelligence for planning and coordinating attacks. It offers:

- easy access
- little or no regulation, censorship, or other forms of government control
- potentially huge audiences spread throughout the world
- anonymity of communication
- fast flow of information
- inexpensive development and maintenance of a web presence
- a multimedia environment—the ability to combine text, graphics, audio, and video
- the ability to shape coverage in the traditional mass media, which increasingly use the internet as a source for stories

DoD has banned the virtual globe, map, and geographic information program, Google Earth, from making detailed street-level video maps of American military bases. In January, 2007, clearly visible Google Earth images of British military bases were discovered in the homes of Iraqi insurgents. The terrorists that attacked numerous locations in India last November used Google Earth's satellite photographs of the city to locate their targets and coordinate their attacks. A petition entered at the Mumbai High Court alleges Google Earth "aids terrorists in plotting attacks." Google Earth routinely offers up digital satellite images of critical installations that, in previous times, would only have been available to government agencies. The real-time status of images depends upon the feature, but because Google Earth is viewed as an effective program to help identify the parts of the US electricity transmission system most vulnerable to extreme weather, terrorists realize an opportunity to exploit.

The Smart Grid Needs to Be Secure

Smart Grid will simultaneously expand the infrastructure for transporting electricity and present a more physically challenging infrastructure to protect. Smart Grid's use of internet technologies makes its full protection prior to deployment a matter of national security, as America's enemies work to exploit all channels of information. Unfortunately, the National Cyber Security Division of DHS has been under fire since its inception and received letter grades of "F" from congressional overseers. Smart Grid risk management involves three crucial steps: 1) assess threats 2) detect vulnerabilities and 3) gauge the risk and identify countermeasures. Locking off potential access points with two-factor authentication systems, for example, includes human factors ("something you are"), personal factors ("something you know"), and technical factors ("something you have").

The Chair of FERC, Jon Wellinghoff has called for "standards to ensure the reliability and security, both physical and cyber, of the electric system." The fact many of the aforementioned intrusions were detected by US intelligence agencies and not by the companies in charge of the infrastructure indicates federal programs to protect computer networks must expand out to the private level. For Smart Grid to be successfully deployed, physical security and cyber security must succeed together, or both will fail.

7

Social, Not Technical, Issues Will Determine Smart Grid Acceptance

David Alan Grier

David Alan Grier is an associate professor of international science and technology policy at George Washington University. He is also a senior member of IEEE, a global collective of professionals dedicated to the advancement of technology.

The proposed "smart grid" promises to change the way electricity is delivered and utilized. The new system will transform consumption and pricing markets that were based on group demand to ones that are driven by individuals. The focus on individual consumers will also mean that utilities can glean a lot of personal information about energy use from customers. These changes will be substantial and unprecedented. Therefore, while the smart grid may require a whole new set of technological innovations to operate, the industry's focus on the individual and society's acceptance of the responsibility of power use (as well as the loss of privacy that may come with it) will determine whether the nation will embrace this new system.

Nothing demands a more detailed accounting of our actions than a roaring prairie fire, a glowing wall of energy that stands ready to take all that we might have to offer. Such fires occasionally occur in the region that holds my family's farm, a picturesque 12 acres in the dry foothills of the American West.

David Alan Grier, "Dumb Grids and Smart Markets," *Computer*, vol. 44, no. 6, June 2011, pp. 6–8.

The farm has an emergency electrical generator to provide water to fight the flames. Even a modest fire could cut the connection to the power grid and make it impossible to pump anything from the aquifer that lies some 30 feet below the surface.

The generator can deliver 15 kW [kilowatts] in a matter of seconds, but it can't begin to satisfy the full demand from the farm. The water pump takes almost 3 kW by itself. That load is compounded by the power required by other essential equipment: the air conditioner, barnyard lamps, and hay loader. If you want a hot shower and a cold drink after defeating the fire, you'll need to add a couple more kW for the refrigerator and the water heater. Without an accurate account of the electrical load, the generator will grind to a halt long before you can bring its power to bear on the fire.

More than any other issue, the ideas of aggregation and markets lie behind the current discussions of electrical infrastructure, the discussions that focus on the concept we now call the smart grid.

In that moment before you throw the switch, when the circuits are still part of the local power grid, nobody has to make a detailed load calculation for the farm. The power demand for every family in the hills is aggregated into a single quantity. The local utility cares nothing about your individual needs until it comes time to settle the bill at the end of the month. You might need a little more electricity or your neighbor might require a little less. From the utility's point of view, these fluctuations are lost in the aggregate demand. It manages the local infrastructure for the aggregate, not for the individual. This may not be the most efficient way to manage electrical power, but it has worked fairly well for almost a century.

Individual vs. Aggregate Demand

More than any other issue, the ideas of aggregation and markets lie behind the current discussions of electrical infrastructure, the discussions that focus on the concept we now call the smart grid. We tend to view this as a technological problem. "Using digital sensors, computing modeling and real-time data, a smart grid would revolutionize our antiquated" electrical power system, explained a recent [2011] article in *The New York Times*. Yet, the smart grid really involves a radical change in how we view the market for electrical power, a change that will require us to be more responsible for our own actions and more dependent upon our neighbors.

For most of its history, the power market has involved a dialogue between two parties: centralized generators and aggregate populations. In its earliest days, this dialogue was best described by utility magnate Samuel Insull. After starting his career as an assistant in Thomas Edison's company, Insull launched his own firm to create the large electrical utilities. In forming those utilities, he recognized that aggregate demand was more uniform than the demand from any individual household and thus "the fundamental basis of the profit-making of an energy-selling company."

Insull promoted his ideas with a set of charts and diagrams that became well-known in the early electrical industry. Aggregating demand from small consumers produced a more uniform and predictable demand for electricity, he argued. "The characteristics of an individual are therefore of interest only in that they form a contribution to the characteristics of the group," he explained.

Consequently, "we can sell these small customers at a profit as a whole whereas any engineer who knew the facts could demonstrate to me that each one by himself is a loss to us."

The financial markets lavishly rewarded Insull's ideas. His utilities were the largest and best financed of his age. He used these resources to build the control structure that we currently associate with electrical markets. This structure divided the electrical supply into three parts: generation, transmission, and distribution. He moved generation into large, centralized plants because they were more efficient. By contrast, his competitors were generally building regional or neighborhood plants.

To aggregate demand, Insull created large distribution grids that were controlled by regional substations. These stations kept statistics on electrical usage, projected demand, and monitored the actual consumption of power. The stations were connected to generators and to one another by dedicated phone lines. The stations could use these phones to call for additional power or report that the demand for electricity wasn't as great as anticipated.

As currently conceived, the smart grid will bring us the tools to start thinking about individual electrical consumption rather than aggregate consumption.

The last element, the transmission lines, linked generators to grids. Initially, the utilities owned these lines as well as the grids and generators. However, by slow and steady steps, they became part of a market for bulk electricity. By the 1930s, this market included the generators in government hydroelectric projects. By the late 1970s, it had expanded to embrace a substantial collection of government, private, and public entities. However, this market still operated according to Samuel Insull's principle of aggregate demand.

A New Principle for Electric Markets

As currently conceived, the smart grid will bring us the tools to start thinking about individual electrical consumption rather than aggregate consumption. Just as social networking has given people the ability to exchange ideas as individuals rather than as members of institutions, the smart grid allows entities to participate in the electrical markets as individuals. These markets will provide new information for controlling the grids, calling for power from transmission lines, and ultimately projecting the requirements for electrical generation.

The proponents of smart grids argue that this approach to power management will let them accommodate new technologies, such as electric automobiles. The "idle capacity of today's electric power grid," reports a study by the Department of Energy, "could supply 70 percent of the energy needs of today's cars and light trucks without adding to generation or transmission capacity—if the vehicles charged during off-peak times."

The task of building a smart grid requires us to solve two kinds of problems: technical and social.

This aspect of the smart grid discussion parallels the ideas of Insull, who used statistical methodology to incorporate the demand from electrical railroads into his utilities. "If you consider it merely as a fraction of the supply of energy required by a community for all kinds of purposes," he observed, "the demand from railroads is found to be simply an incident."

Technical and Social Problems

The task of building a smart grid requires us to solve two kinds of problems: technical and social. Of these two classes, the technical problems may be easiest to address. Much of the fundamental technology is based on well-tested ideas, such as those found in the Internet's hardware and software. Some have called for radically new technology to support the smart grid, including new means for transmitting and storing power. However, most of the research builds on existing technology.

By contrast, addressing the social and managerial problems may be much more difficult. Many of these problems come from the segmented structure of the nation's electrical infrastructure. Although this infrastructure involves several large government entities, such as the generation plants of the Bureau of Land Reclamation or the Tennessee Valley Authority, local agencies control most of the system. As they should, these local agencies consider only their own interests when they make policy. As a consequence, they tend to reject plans that require them to make sacrifices on behalf of the greater good. This is perhaps best illustrated by the problems of building new transmission facilities. "It is becoming increasingly difficult to site new conventional overhead transmission lines," explained a recent US government report, "particularly in urban and suburban areas experiencing the greatest load growth."

The task of focusing investment on the right aspects of the smart grid will be tricky . . .

Yet, the construction of new facilities is only one aspect of the social problem. The plans for the smart grid propose an infrastructure that can operate in a unified manner. Such plans will require large investments and force the public debate to concentrate on the problem of controlling financial risk rather than on the value of radical innovation. No one, as Samuel Insull knew well, wants an expensive infrastructure, no matter how large a market it creates, if that infrastructure has a high risk of creating a financial loss.

Investment, Information, and Privacy Concerns

The task of focusing investment on the right aspects of the smart grid will be tricky, as the new electrical infrastructure might create markets that can't deliver all the benefits their supporters claim. Many reports note that the smart grid will be able to handle new suppliers as well as consumers: thus, any small investor could purchase a generator and add power to the network. However, that idea will work only if the market can set a price that will reward small investments. The current electrical infrastructure can't reward a family that wants to put solar cells on its roof or chooses to place a spinning turbine next to its barn. It's far from obvious that the smart grid will do a better job of providing incentives to such projects unless it substantially increases the price of electricity.

If markets run on information and if bad information can destroy markets, then the markets that the smart grid forms will need to protect their data streams.

Any market can, of course, be shaped by initial investment, technical and operational standards, subsidies, and early demonstrations. Currently, much of the technical work on the smart grid involves these issues. "The Smart Grid will ultimately require hundreds of standards, specifications, and requirements," explains a report by the National Institute of Standards and Technology [NIST]. In addition to standards, NIST is creating a plan—a road map—to shape the industry and encourage investment. The Department of Energy is supporting research to develop the smart grid's basic technical elements. Agencies in Europe and Japan are addressing similar issues as they work to create their own version of the smart grid.

Among those hundreds of specifications and requirements, one item is repeatedly identified as central to the task of creating a smart grid: securing network information. If markets run on information and if bad information can destroy markets, then the markets that the smart grid forms will need to protect their data streams. "Cyber security must address not only deliberate attacks, such as from disgruntled employees, industrial espionage, and terrorists," notes the NIST report, "but also inadvertent compromises of the information infrastructure due to user errors, equipment failures, and natural disasters."

With almost 25 years of experience in dealing with the problems of data security, we've learned that cyber attacks can embarrass organizations, damage credit ratings, disrupt government operations (as such attacks did in Estonia), and destroy industrial machinery (as seems to have been the case with the recent Stuxnet malware). Records of electrical usage may not be as sensitive as our medical history or our credit information, but they still build an intimate record of our lives. The utilities know when we're sleeping, and they know when we're awake. They know when we watch television or open the refrigerator to cheat on our diet. Conceivably, they'll know about the unexpected trip that requires us to charge the electric automobile.

No One Knows What the New Market Will Bring

Of course, we have a long experience with trading information for better industrial products and more efficient services. Overall, the exchange seems to have been beneficial, producing more value than it has claimed. Still, we don't really know all the ramifications of living in a more active and individualized electricity market. It might have little impact upon our day-to-day lives or put us in a position of revealing to our neighbors more details than we'd like them to know.

Even though he managed his utilities with aggregate statistics, Samuel Insull would certainly have wanted to know more about his customers. "At his fingertips," noted one biographer, "he always had an impressive array of statistical data." He argued that the value a community received from a stable source of electrical power was well worth the cost of the information. As Insull explained in 1912, "There is no greater problem in the industrial world today than the proper method of producing energy and distributing it in a given area."

8

Remote Energy Management Systems Can Help to Control Energy

Sarah Reedy

Sarah Reedy is a senior editor at Connected Planet, *a technology network publication.*

Various telecommunications companies are experimenting with remote energy management (REM) tools that will enable these businesses to fuse telecommunication services with energy use monitoring programs. Decades before any proposed "smart grid" is up and running, these forward-thinking enterprises are looking to partner with utilities to make remote energy management a reality. Such partnerships are likely to grow in coming years because they offer load management ability for utilities, reduce energy bills for consumers, and generate a source of income for telecom companies.

In-home energy management is a cornerstone of the smart grid movement, but it's not necessarily reliant on having the updated grid infrastructure and demand response technology in place. There are a host of players, including telcos, IT [internet technology] companies, hardware- and software-makers, exploring remote energy management [REM] services on a number of interfaces spanning the mobile phone, PC, television and, eventually, the smart meter.

The utilities ultimately will be responsible for issuing the smart meters, thermostats and other equipment that enable

REM, as well as incorporating them into their existing infrastructure, but telcos have an opportunity to offer products and services to that utility, said Larry Fisher, next-gen research director for ABI Research. After last week's [November, 2009] granting of the smart grid stimulus funds, many companies are already beginning to explore how to partner up with the utilities moving forward on projects.

"With the smart grid money beginning to flow in earnest, hardware and networking vendors will step up their marketing at the utilities," Fisher said in an e-mail interview. "Google is a good example; the company has been working to build relationships with utilities and with independent device manufacturers based on its PowerMeter, a software tool that can show consumers their home energy consumption data in near-real time."

While to date, most telcos involvement in REM has been through a host of mobile apps, they are also exploring the opportunity to offer services either direct to the consumer or the utility.

Google is working with smart meter-maker Itron and energy device-maker AlertMe, to ensure its service will work with equipment utilities are actually installing on customer premises, Fisher said. Ten utilities in various stages of their smart grid rollouts are also testing the service with Google. Fellow IT heavyweight Microsoft is also trialing a service, Hohm, with utilities. The free online app focuses on personalized energy savings recommendations based on information that either the consumer or their utility provides about the home's layout and appliance usage.

Telecommunications Companies Already Offer Some "Smart" Services

While to date, most telcos involvement in REM has been through a host of mobile apps, they are also exploring the opportunity to offer services either direct to the consumer or the utility. As triple-play providers, telcos like Verizon and AT&T have the opportunity to leverage REM through their IPTV [Internet Protocol television] or broadband packages. Like other interactive applications they are trialing on the TV, REM could be another service tied to their middleware. AT&T is also exploring ways to allow consumers to more easily utilize the data coming off their appliances, such as over a gateway or router in the home that could alert the mobile device if an appliance stopped functioning, said Chris Hill, vice president of mobility product management for AT&T Business Solutions.

Networking chip-maker Ember uses a mesh network to scale and machine-to-machine (M2M) communications to enable connections between devices in the home, including smart meters. CEO Bob LeFort is seeing increased interest from telcos in providing value-added energy awareness and management services on top of their existing content in the home. He expects deployments early next year.

"If you don't have a smart meter, you can put [a collar] around the incoming electric wires and using the principals of electro-magnetism, you can calculate the electricity being used on the collar," LeFort said. "The hub would plug into your Ethernet port and there would be a low-cost display. That's the baseline package, and [telcos] are able to disaggregate your energy usage, so by having the energy coming into your house and using some smart logic, they can help you do things like, for instance, per rate all your energy usage. What are the biggest energy users in your home—your fridge, TV, cable set-top box. This allows you to be, one, more aware, but also more knowledgeable and have seamless control of how you use your energy."

Consumers Lack Interest in Expensive Services

Despite the enthusiasm in the industry, it's not a given that consumers are even interested in having that level of control in their home. This year's Green Power Progress Survey found that consumers would pay only about $48 to install hardware to monitor and manage energy usage. The same respondents said on average that they would pay $13 per month for the service with 30% unwilling to pay anything and 19% indicating they'd pay more than $20.

For this reason, most REM apps are offered free to consumers today. Fisher said this could change as higher consumer fees are required to defray the costs of implementing smart meters. Once those costs are recouped, he said that utilities will be able to reduce their fees and offer consumers energy management capabilities as a value-added service, but one that likely has a monthly fee attached. Another way utilities can help consumers with the fees is in conjunction with their homeowner's insurance, said Paul Dawes, CEO of broadband home management company iControl Networks.

Despite the enthusiasm in the industry, it's not a given that consumers are even interested in having that level of control in their home.

"If you are paying $35 for home security, you are getting 10 or 20% off of homeowner's insurance, which is saving you—depending on the cost—$10 to $20 a month," Dawes said. "With energy management, you can save another $10 to $20 a month. You end up with a service that a consumer is paying for, but the net cost to them is zero or even positive." Right now, Dawes said that energy management is a set of features that consumers will gladly adopt, but they won't pay for the privilege. As such, it should be part of an entire home management package, he said. For energy, specifically, what people want is to know how much they are using and how they can save energy in a format that is easy to understand and to implement. Simply pushing a button to arm a REM system is the extent of what most will want to do, he said.

LaForte echoed the need for a simple, transparent system and suggested a lighting display in which green means energy is cheap, yellow means the expense is creeping up, red means avoid use if possible and blinking red means avoid use at all costs. Consumers don't have to adhere to the system, but at least the options are clear.

Making REM a Win-Win Situation

Based on the nature of the smart grid and REM, in particular, privacy concerns will continue to be a hurdle in offering these services. Fisher said written consumer buy-in will likely be required in order to enable next-generation information services based on smart grid upgrades, as well as any information-sharing with other services. There are also issues that still need to be fleshed out around flows of information: how much information a utility gives up and who owns that consumer relationship. If a mutually beneficial middle ground is reached, however, it can be a win-win scenario for all the parties involved.

"You can imagine a Comcast or Verizon going to PG&E [Pacific Gas & Electric] and saying, 'Hey we have 600,000 subscribers in your footprint that all have smart thermostats, and we can control those systems, and they are willing to sign up for an energy demand response program from you,'" Dawes said. "The utility will, in many cases, be willing to pay the broadband operator for that access. The consumers who opt in will get a lower energy bill, the utilities get to save money on energy costs from managing their load more efficiently, and the broadband operators can draw more revenue or reduce the fees they charge a subscriber because it's being subsidized by the utility."

9

Electric Car Batteries Could Provide Energy Storage for the Smart Grid

Ethan Goffman

Ethan Goffman is an environmental journalist living in Maryland who specializes in energy issues.

Electric cars will not only save on fossil fuel use and carbon emissions, they will become important elements in the proposed "smart grid" that will monitor and regulate energy distribution in the United States. Electric cars will charge when the grid indicates power demand and pricing is low, and their batteries can be tapped when demand is high. In this manner, idle cars might be used collectively as energy providers, pumping electricity back into the grid at peak hours. As remote renewable energy sources become a primary contributor to the energy grid, the power used by these cars may be entirely sustainable and environmentally friendly.

Coupled with a growing fleet of hybrid electric, and eventually fully electric, vehicles, the smart grid could save massive amounts of power, enable alternative energy and be a potent weapon in the fight against climate change. But the question of how best to integrate alternative energy options is tricky. Wind and solar are intermittent. Electric cars rely on an expensive battery and need time to power up. Maximizing alternative energy requires a new kind of intelligence and flexibility.

Ethan Goffman, "Smart and Smarter," *E: The Environmental Magazine*, vol. 21, no. 4, July/August 2010. pp. 30–31.

Fortunately, that dynamic mix should soon be available in the form of a smart grid that's able to deliver electricity with pinpoint efficiency. Electric vehicles will take in electricity when the rates are lowest. Even better is the possibility that such vehicles will then return electricity to the grid when it's most needed. A smart grid would essentially "let the grid reach down and optimize delivery," says Allen Hefner, a scientist on the Smart Grid Team at the National Institute of Standards and Technology.

Charging Cars at Night

In one likely scenario, plug-in vehicles would power their batteries late at night when demand is low. Then, when demand is high, hundreds of thousands of vehicles would return energy to the grid as needed. Institute of Electrical and Electronics Engineer Fellow Alan Mantooth describes "a nine-story garage full of electric vehicles" that he says will function "as one big battery."

Storage has long been a problem for alternative energy, given that solar power can be disrupted by clouds and is unavailable at night, and wind might die down when most needed. The use of plug-in vehicles as storage units, regulated by a smart grid, would thus provide tremendous flexibility, squeezing more out of alternative energy.

Such a scenario "demands a certain level of study," says Mantooth, "to come up with charging/discharge algorithms." Because a battery pack for an electric car costs upwards of $10,000, the possibility that recurrent charging and discharging would wear out the battery remains a problem. The hope is for a resilient battery capable of performing long-term under a variety of conditions. While studies are not complete, anecdotal data on the hybrid electric Toyota Prius shows that "batteries have been holding up nicely," says Mantooth. Another factor is how slowly or quickly batteries charge and discharge energy, with a quick-charge battery the most flexible option to date.

Smart grid users would have control over when their car takes in energy, for instance setting it to charge only at times of minimum costs, if they know their vehicle is to be parked for a long time, or to charge quickly despite cost if they'll need it soon. "If everyone plugs in their vehicles at 5 p.m., the grid can't take it," says Hefner. Instead, charging can be "staggered over a long period of time."

[W]hen demand is high, hundreds of thousands of vehicles would return energy to the grid as needed.

Renewable Energy Is a Key Factor

Two kinds of plug-in vehicles are now or will shortly be available. Hybrid electric cars that depend on a gasoline engine for extended range will include the Fisker Karma, the Chevy Volt and a new version of the Toyota Prius. Fully electric cars include the already-available Tesla Roadster and the Nissan Leaf.

Hybrid and electric cars are only a real environmental step up if coupled with greater use of alternative energy. Mantooth points out that the possibility of switching to 100 million electric cars in the U.S., if tied to an electric system based largely on coal, as we have today, would be "trading one problem for another." Renewable energy dispatched through a smart grid, conversely, would be "a big net plus for electrical efficiency and reduction of greenhouse gases."

Two experimental projects are already combining electric vehicles and the smart grid. Toyota, in partnership with Xcel Energy, is supplying about 20 hybrid electric Priuses to SmartGridCity, a working prototype of the future located in Boulder, Colorado. While SmartGridCity was launched in 2008, the electric car part of the program is set to begin by July of this year.

Beyond technology, the program is testing "a lot of other social and behavioral questions," says Jaycie Chitwood, future fuels and environmental strategy manager at Toyota. "One of the goals has been to incentivize customers to balance the load between charges, peaks and valleys."

Smart grid users would have control over when their car takes in energy, for instance setting it to charge only at times of minimum costs.

Building a Charging Grid

But SmartGridCity still has a problem—car batteries will be charged primarily from homes. "There aren't any public stations yet, say in hotels or underground parking," says Chitwood. "Right now there's not a lot of that in Boulder or anywhere." Furthermore, interaction is one-way, with cars taking power from the grid but not able to return it, and to act as storage batteries.

To begin to put a broader infrastructure into place, the Electric Transportation Engineering Corporation, eTec, is working on the EV Project, funded by a $100 million grant from the U.S. Department of Energy, to bring charging stations to five states: Arizona, California, Oregon, Tennessee and Washington. Some 11,000 charging stations are projected. While most will rely on the grid, 125 will be equipped with solar panels to provide energy from the sun directly to cars. According to Burak Ozpineci, leader of the Power and Energy Systems Group at Oak Ridge National Laboratory (ORNL), "these charging stations will be like gas stations" for electric cars.

As part of this effort, a pilot project with 100 charging stations is to be installed in December 2010 on the Tennessee campus of ORNL. Participants will drive the Nissan Leaf, a 100% electric vehicle. Twenty-five of the charging stations will be solar, allowing a driving experience free of gasoline, coal or other fossil fuels. Nevertheless, as with SmartGridCity, the project will not allow cars to put electricity back into the grid. No vehicles near production have that capability, according to Ozpineci.

To begin to put a broader infrastructure into place, the Electric Transportation Engineering Corporation, eTec, is working on the EV Project, funded by a $100 million grant from the U.S. Department of Energy . . .

The project will also study how to implement electric cars in a smart grid setting as used by actual human beings. "It hasn't been done," says Ozpineci. "We're trying to come up with best practices," he adds, including such mundane details as keeping people from tripping over power cords. The project will closely monitor habits, such as how often, at what times and at what levels consumers charge their vehicles. Another option being studied is whether consumers might have an extra battery at home to be charged while the vehicle is on the road.

A Gradual Conversion

Hefner believes that everything is in place to begin the evolution toward hybrid electric, and then fully electric cars coupled to a smart grid. Businesses are taking the initiatives that could build into a complete system. "The infrastructure can evolve," he says. "We don't need to replace every gasoline station now." Hybrid electrics could at first charge up only at home, then at select parking lots and eventually at roadside stations.

But the viability of converting to a combination of electric cars and a smart grid depends largely on the cost of the alternative: today's gasoline. If the "price of gas is at $2 a gallon, this ain't gonna happen," says Mantooth. "But at $4.50 a gallon, this will happen."

Of course, the price of gas could be artificially increased if a carbon tax is instituted. As Hefner points out, "the cost of delivering service can include social costs such as carbon dioxide emissions."

10

The Smart Grid Must Be Adopted or Global Civilization Will Fail

Laurent Liscia

Laurent Liscia is the executive director of OASIS (Organization for the Advancement of Structured Information Standards), a nonprofit advocacy collective that promotes the development and adoption of open (public, no fee) standards for global information networks.

Because the world is running out of oil—a dominant fossil fuel—humanity will have to rethink the way it produces and uses energy. The "smart grid" is the visionary means of bringing renewable energy sources into the production cycle while allowing individuals to control their energy use and even create surplus energy to feed back into the grid. If the world does not adopt this new power network, human civilization will stagnate and collapse. The way forward is clear: people must rid themselves of fossil fuel consumption and embrace the new system in which individuals and power companies are partners in producing energy and controlling its use.

I saw [Microsoft regional director and software pioneer] Juval Lowy in a magnificent, long and somewhat breathless prophetic exercise compare the Smart Grid to the Internet. In his view, the set of new devices and protocols that promise to make the Grid orders of magnitude smarter than it is today will seed a cloud of new startups from which the giants of tomorrow will emerge. Or to be precise, a few winners will rise from the wreckage of thousands. He's right, if only because this is a modern page from [Austrian-American economist Joseph] Schumpeter's scroll on creative destruction[1].

The analogy has obvious limitations: the Internet is a medium for content, the Grid is not. And while the Internet has infinitely multiplied our ability to shop for coasters, make vapid statements about ourselves, stay obsessively in touch, post bad pictures for the world not to look at, and sure, grow more productive; the Smart Grid will "only" impact the way we deal with power sources.

Beyond the limitations, what is true about the analogy between the Smart Grid and the Internet is what has not been said about it.

[T]he Smart Grid will happen quickly because without it, we will fail as a civilization, and we run the very real risk of devolving.

A Prophecy or Doomed Prediction?

Please bear with me as I seem to indulge in a philosophical aside on the precarious nature of prognostication. I remember reading, as a young man, George Gilder's *Microcosm*, a chronicle of the "quantum" triumph of the microchip and its profound impact on the world economy. Gilder's thinking was (and remains) utterly brilliant as long as it made sense of what had already taken place, but lost its sharp definition as it attempted to chart the imminent future, which, predictably, failed to occur as sketched. That is the only predictable trait of predictions: they very seldom come true. The reason for this is the forced shortsightedness that comes with living in the present.

1. The popular belief that economic progress arises from innovation unleashed by a few visionary entrepreneurs.

And so I will make my own doomed prediction, based on a true premise: the Smart Grid is like the Internet because the potential of its economic engine is equally staggering. (Well, I suppose that's a bit of a prediction right there). And now for the prophecy: the Smart Grid will happen quickly because without it, we will fail as a civilization, and we run the very real risk of devolving. This has to do with the phenomenon of "Peak Oil": the idea that we have discovered more usable fossil fuels fields than there are still to be found. . . .

[S]hould [power companies] unwisely choose not to embrace the smarter grid, their survival will be in question.

Corollary: the writing is on the wall for us as a species if we do not solve the energy conundrum. There is a common concept in science-fiction that describes species so old and mature that they end up "subliming", vanishing into an incomprehensible nirvana of their own making. This posits that cultural and biological evolution become one. I believe we are witnessing this on a planetary scale: the challenges that face us are not about nations, they are about humankind as a whole. We all feel this, but we do not know it in our minds—we are still attached to our flags, our heritage, our neck of the woods. And yet, the knowledge is here for all to acquire: global warming; global water shortages; global terrorism; globalization (notice the repetition). If we cannot successfully navigate these challenges, we will inevitably fail as a global culture. We may even peter out as an evolutionary branch, leaving the playing field to the raccoons, the coyotes and the social insects.

Individuals Making Real Choices

Smart Grid will help us meet the challenges. It is a surefire way of drastically reducing our consumption of energy; of making the energy markets drastically more efficient; of putting the responsibility for energy usage squarely in the hands of those it affects the most: you and I. And this is where recent history offers us insights, and where the analogy between the Internet and Smart Grid revolutions finds another parallel: when the telephone companies were deregulated, at first there was tohu and bohu, and lo and behold, from this chaos emerged reconstructed telephone empires. The true deregulation occurred only when digital and cellular changed the game: the Internet brought us and continues us to bring us real choice. In the same way, the utility deregulation first brought us chaos, blackouts, governor recalls and insane prices. The true deregulation will happen when the Smart Grid brings new energy producers on the scene. Anyone with solar panels on their roof is a producer! Of course today's utilities will be players; but not the only players. And should they unwisely choose not to embrace the smarter grid, their survival will be in question.

The title of this post was incorrect after all. The Smart Grid MUST happen or the world may change in ways that we do not want to experience.

You can be part of the change by joining our OASIS Blue initiative. OASIS Blue will speed up the advent of SmartGrid by making all the devices that compose it interoperable. Panels will talk to TVs, Fridges will talk to the Grid; you will buy and sell power from your house computer, and there will be a need for a language that all these pieces understand: a set of standards.

Welcome to the future.

11

Energy Solutions in Developing Countries Bypass the Traditional Grid Model

The Economist

The Economist *is a weekly British newspaper that focuses on international business and politics. The publication eschews personalized bylines so that the entire newspaper can speak with a unified voice.*

More than a billion people worldwide lack access to electricity. Instead of waiting for a modern electrical grid to reach these potential consumers, entrepreneurs are devising local solutions to power supply and distribution in these largely poor regions of the globe. Using biofuels, solar energy, and other means, small businesses are springing up to bring affordable electricity to those who cannot pay much for its use. Lack of financing is the chief hurdle limiting the growth of these micro-operations and distribution networks. However, the entrepreneurial spirit is strong in developing nations, and the customer demand is encouraging, suggesting that the bottom-up approach may succeed where planned electrical grids have yet to reach.

Around 1.5 billion people, or more than a fifth of the world's population, have no access to electricity, and a billion more have only an unreliable and intermittent supply. Of the people without electricity, 85% live in rural areas or on the fringes of cities. Extending energy grids into these areas is

The Economist, "Power to the People," vol. 396, September 4, 2010. pp. 23-24.

expensive: the United Nations estimates that an average of $35 billion–40 billion a year needs to be invested until 2030 so everyone on the planet can cook, heat and light their premises, and have energy for productive uses such as schooling. On current trends, however, the number of "energy poor" people will barely budge, and 16% of the world's population will still have no electricity by 2030, according to the International Energy Agency.

But why wait for top-down solutions? Providing energy in a bottom-up way instead has a lot to recommend it. There is no need to wait for politicians or utilities to act. The technology in question, from solar panels to low-energy light-emitting diodes (LEDs), is rapidly falling in price. Local, bottom-up systems may be more sustainable and produce fewer carbon emissions than centralised schemes. In the rich world, in fact, the trend is towards a more flexible system of distributed, sustainable power sources. The developing world has an opportunity to leapfrog the centralised model, just as it leapfrogged fixed-line telecoms and went straight to mobile phones.

Solar cells can be used to power low-energy LEDs, which are both energy-efficient and cheap . . .

But just as the spread of mobile phones was helped along by new business models, such as pre-paid airtime cards and village "telephone ladies", new approaches are now needed. "We need to reinvent how energy is delivered," says Simon Desjardins, who manages a programme at the Shell Foundation that invests in for-profit ways to deliver energy to the poor. "Companies need to come up with innovative business models and technology." Fortunately, lots of people are doing just that.

The Spread of Solar Power and LEDs

Start with lighting, which prompted the establishment of the first electrical utilities in the rich world. At the "Lighting Africa" conference in Nairobi in May [2010], a World Bank project to encourage private-sector solutions for the poor, 50 lighting firms displayed their wares, up from just a handful last year. This illustrates both the growing interest in bottom-up solutions and falling prices. Prices of solar cells have also fallen, so that the cost per kilowatt is half what it was a decade ago. Solar cells can be used to power low-energy LEDs, which are both energy-efficient and cheap: the cost of a set of LEDs to light a home has fallen by half in the past decade, and is now below $25.

It is not just new technology that is needed, but new [supply and distribution] models.

"This could eliminate kerosene lighting in the next ten years, the way cellphones took off in about 13 years," says Richenda Van Leeuwen of the Energy Access Initiative at the UN Foundation in Washington, DC. That would have a number of benefits: families in the developing world may spend as much as 30% of their income on kerosene, and kerosene lighting causes indoor air pollution and fires.

But such systems are still beyond the reach of the very poorest. "There are hundreds of millions who can afford clean energy, but there is still a barrier for the billions who cannot," says Sam Goldman, the chief executive of D.light. His firm has developed a range of solar-powered systems that can provide up to 12 hours of light after charging in sunlight for one day. D.light's most basic solar lantern costs $10. But the price would have to fall below $5 to make it universally affordable, according to a study by the International Finance Corporation, an arm of the World Bank. So there is scope for further improvement.

Biofuels in Rural Areas

It is not just new technology that is needed, but new models. Much of the ferment in bottom-up energy entrepreneurialism is focusing on South Asia, where 570m people in India, Pakistan and Bangladesh, mostly in rural areas, have no access to electricity, according to the International Energy Agency. One idea is to use locally available biomass as a feedstock to generate power for a village-level "micro-grid". Husk Power Systems, an Indian firm, uses second-world-war-era diesel generators fitted with biomass gasifiers that can use rice husks, which are otherwise left to rot, as a feedstock. Wires are strung on cheap, easy-to-repair bamboo poles to provide power to around 600 families for each generator. Co-founded three years ago by a local electrical engineer, Gyanesh Pandey, Husk has established five mini-grids in Bihar, India's poorest state, where rice is a staple crop. It hopes to extend its coverage to 50 mini-grids during 2010. Consumers pay door-to-door collectors upfront for power, and Husk collects a 30% government subsidy for construction costs. Its pilot plants were profitable within six months, so its model is sustainable.

Emergence BioEnergy takes this approach a step farther. Its aim is to provide many entrepreneurial opportunities around energy production, says Iqbal Quadir, the firm's founder, who is also director of the Legatum Centre for Development & Entrepreneurship at the Massachusetts Institute of Technology (MIT). A cattle farmer in a small village in Bangladesh might, for example, operate a one-kilowatt generator in his hut, powered by methane from cow manure stored in his basement. He can then sell surplus electricity to his neighbours and use the waste heat from the generator to run a refrigerator to chill milk. This preserves milk that otherwise might be spoilt, offers new sources of income to the farmer (selling power and other services, such as charging mobile phones or running an internet kiosk) and provides power to others in his village.

Energy Entrepreneurship

The farmer funds all this with a microfinance loan. It is no coincidence that this is a similar model to the "telephone lady" scheme, pioneered in Bangladesh a few years ago, in which women use microloans to buy mobile phones and then sell access, by the call, to other villagers; Mr Quadir helped establish Grameenphone, now the largest mobile operator in Bangladesh, and hopes to repeat its success in energy. After a pilot project in two villages, Emergence BioEnergy plans a broader roll-out in 2011 in conjunction with BRAC, a giant microfinance and development NGO [non-governmental organization].

Another project, in India, aims to convert women from gathering wood, which denudes forests, to using canisters of liquefied petroleum gas (LPG). India's four state-owned regional power companies, including Bharat Petroleum Corporation, will build a national network of thousands of LPG-powered community kitchens. Local entrepreneurs will then provide the LPG and charge villagers to use the kitchens in 15-minute increments.

A cattle farmer in a small village in Bangladesh might, for example, operate a one-kilowatt generator in his hut, powered by methane from cow manure stored in his basement.

Harish Hande, managing director of Selco Solar, a social enterprise in India that promotes the adoption of new energy technologies, says the important thing is not so much to deliver energy to the poor, but to provide new ways to generate income. His firm has devised a solar-powered sewing machine, for example. Last year Mr Hande started an incubation lab in rural Karnataka, in southern India, to bring together local customers and engineering interns from MIT, Stanford and Imperial College, London. The lab is currently piloting a hybrid banana dryer that runs on biomass during wet spells and sunlight on dry days to make packets of dried banana—so that farmers no longer have to rely on selling their crop immediately.

Funding and Distribution Obstacles

Even when new technology and models are available, the logistics of rolling them out can be daunting. The two big challenges are providing the upfront investment for energy schemes, and building and maintaining the necessary distribution systems to enable them to reach sufficient scale. At the moment, most schemes are funded by angel investors, foundations and social venture-capital funds. There is a vigorous debate about whether the private sector on its own can make these models work as technology improves, or whether non-profit groups are needed to fill the gaps in funding and distribution.

Microfinance institutions may seem the natural financial partners to help the poor pay for energy systems, since they are the only organisations with millions of poor customers. But teething problems are formidable and success stories are few, says Patrick Maloney of the Lemelson Foundation, which invests in clean-energy technologies for the poor. A telephone lady could buy a mobile phone for a relatively small sum, and would immediately have a source of income with which to repay the loan. Although a household that buys a solar lamp saves money on kerosene, the investment takes several months to pay for itself, and there is no actual income from the lamp. For bigger energy projects, such as micro-generators, the loan required is much larger, and therefore riskier, than the loan for a mobile phone.

Moreover, microfinance institutions may lack the funds to identify reliable energy suppliers, educate loan officers about clean-energy technologies and build a support network for energy schemes. One way to solve this problem, being pursued by MicroEnergy Credits, a social enterprise, is to plug microfinance institutions into carbon markets. Projects can then be funded by selling carbon credits when a microfinance customer switches from kerosene to solar lighting, for example.

Distribution is also a problem, particularly in Africa and South Asia, where the majority of the world's energy-poor live. Infrastructure and supply chains are poor or non-existent, particularly in rural areas. Recruiting and training a sales force, and educating consumers of the benefits of switching away from wood or kerosene, must be paid for somehow. Social enterprises are innovating in this area, too. Solar Aid, a non-profit group, specialises in setting up microfranchises to identify and train entrepreneurs. The organisation works with local authorities to identify potential entrepreneurs, who must gather signatures from their local community—providing both the endorsement of their neighbours and a future customer base. They then undergo five days of training with an exam at the end. Solar Aid is also testing a kiosk-based system to help entrepreneurs distribute LED lighting in the Kibera district of the Kenyan capital, Nairobi.

The two big challenges are providing the upfront investment for energy schemes, and building and maintaining the necessary distribution systems to enable them to reach sufficient scale.

Some hurdles to bottom-up energy projects are more easily addressed. In particular, high import duties on clean-energy products in many developing countries, notably in Africa, hamper their adoption by the poor. Ethiopia, for example, imposes a 100% duty on imports of solar products, while Malawi charges a 47.5% tax on LED lighting systems. Such taxes are sometimes defended on the basis that only the rich can afford fancy technology. But the same was said about mobile phones a decade ago—and look at them now.

12

Living off the Grid Reduces Impact on Plants and Increases Independence

Cam Mather

Cam Mather is a writer who advocates living sustainably without being connected to traditional power networks. He is the author of Thriving During Challenging Times *and* The All You Can Eat Gardening Handbook.

Instead of waiting for a "smart grid" to bring cheaper renewable energy to everyone, people should consider living off the grid, producing their own energy to fit their needs. Equipping homes with solar cells and wind turbines can help reduce utility bills and, perhaps eventually, cut one off entirely from the public network. Using sustainable wood for heating fuel can also reduce one's carbon footprint. Such changes will make everyone more self-sufficient and cut down on greenhouse gas emissions that have led to climate change.

More than a decade ago, my wife, Michelle, and I moved from a busy suburban street to 150 acres in the Ontario bush, where our nearest neighbors are three miles away. Ditto for the nearest utility pole. We moved off the grid with little knowledge about renewable energy—or electricity, for that matter—and had to quickly put into practice our homeschooling mantra of "lifelong learning."

To say that the learning curve was steep is an understatement. Back then, there were no good books on the subject of

Cam Mather, "Off the Grid and Thriving," *Mother Earth News*, vol. 238, February/March 2010, pp. 83–87.

renewable energy for homes, and the information you could find was pieced together by pioneers who were learning as they went along. Consulting with any local electrician was a waste of time, so we learned by the seat of our pants. Luckily, we developed a network of helpful and skilled friends along the way. We came to realize that the more things we learned to do ourselves, the more independent we would become, which is the theme of the book I've just written, *Thriving During Challenging Times: The Energy, Food and Financial Independence Handbook.*

[G]enerating your own electricity from the sun and wind provides an incredible sense of well-being . . .

As we begin to experience the converging challenges of resource depletion, climate change and the ongoing financial crisis, we need to make ourselves more resilient to shocks to the system.

Harnessing Renewable Wind and Solar Energy

If you do decide to go off the grid, generating your own electricity from the sun and wind provides an incredible sense of well-being—not only from a sense of independence, but also from the realization that you aren't using any electricity that comes from coal. Powering your home with renewable energy is a huge step toward reducing your carbon footprint. We started with a fairly small solar-electric system that the previous owners of our home had installed, and we've steadily added more panels. As we learned more about peak oil, we were determined to reduce our use of nonrenewable fossil fuels for both cooking and powering our gasoline generator. There are times when there isn't enough sunlight or wind to charge our off-grid batteries, so we use a fossil fuel-powered generator as a backup.

When we moved in, there was an old wind turbine on a 60-foot tower on our property, but several years ago we decided to replace it with a new Bergey 1-kilowatt turbine on a 100-foot tower. We are surrounded by forests (not optimal for wind generation), so putting up a 100-foot tower set the turbine about 30 feet above the trees to capture some of the stronger winds. We decided to film the installation process and sell a video of it via our publishing company, Aztext. I'm a visual learner, and if I could have watched a video of the process of putting all the pieces of our off-the-grid system together, it would have made our efforts go more smoothly.

The new turbine required us to upgrade our battery bank from a 12-volt to a 24-volt system, so we also upgraded our inverter and added more solar panels. In the previous year, we ran our backup generator about 15 times. In the year after we put up the turbine and added solar panels, we ran the generator just twice. This means that, on many days, we now have extra electricity to use for cooking, offsetting our propane use.

Most people who move off grid just move onto propane, substituting propane for all their major heat loads, such as cooking and heating water. We already heat with wood cut sustainably from our property, so using the electric stove helps reduce our propane use as well.

Many utilities now offer incentives to integrate renewable energy technologies [into home energy networks].

The biggest drop in our propane consumption came when we installed our solar hot water system. It uses solar energy to heat water we use for washing and bathing, and should offset about 60 percent of water heating costs. For most people, this should be the first solar panel they put on their roof, because the payback is much faster than that of photovoltaics. There's nothing nicer on a cold winter evening than soaking in a bath with water that was heated all day by the sun. After the system is paid for, there are no additional costs, and there are no carbon dioxide emissions created by the energy that heats the water. It's an incredible, guilt-free luxury.

Many utilities now offer incentives to integrate renewable energy technologies, and with faster paybacks on your investment, you can take the savings from these systems and pay down debt. This was one of our keys to being able to move where we did. We scrimped, saved and paid off our old mortgage before we left the city. Financial independence allows you to capitalize on the opportunities that will present themselves in the future.

Planting a Garden

Living off the grid is just one way of becoming independent, but even if you are connected, you can still make yourself more self-reliant. The final step on our path to independence was creating a vegetable garden. We have sandy soil, but discovered that the area around the old barn foundation had good topsoil. I started by turning over pieces of sod to create the garden, but eventually got smart and purchased rotten hay that I spread on the areas where I wanted to expand the garden. The hay killed the grass, and as it rotted, it added organic matter to the soil. After six to nine months with the hay on the soil, I could rototill the hay in and be ready to plant.

Most people have a sense that the money they spend on food continues to go up, and even though Americans only spend about 10 percent of their income on food (versus up to 90 percent in other parts of the world!), the percentage continues to rise.

We continue to increase the amount of space we devote to potatoes in our garden. The United Nations declared 2008 the "Year of the Potato" because potatoes provide exceptional nutrition and are a rugged plant that grows well in most places.

We have a neighbor who keeps as supplied with extra horse manure to supplement the garden, but there's no reason you can't do just as well in the city. Most municipalities now have pickup for grass clippings and leaves, which are a fantastic source of free organic material for your garden. You just need a wheelbarrow on the night before garbage day to retrieve some for composting.

There's something extremely liberating about cooking your food without a bill from a utility or a grocery store.

Last year, after upgrading our electrical system, we added a new 10-cubic-foot freezer, which is a big step for someone living off the grid. Luckily our basement isn't heated, so the freezer is in a very cool environment and doesn't consume much electricity. Over the winter, when we're making less electricity from the sun, the basement is so cool that the freezer rarely turns on.

As we've upgraded our system, we've moved more of our cooking requirements to our free homemade electricity. It started with an electric kettle and toaster. Then we added a convection toaster oven, and recently an induction burner, which uses significantly less electricity than a typical resistance electric burner. There's something extremely liberating about cooking your food without a bill from a utility or a grocery store.

A Rewarding Experience

As I look to the future I see a more carbon-constrained world, especially as several billion people in China and India get off their bikes and into cars, so this year we purchased an electric bike. Its lithium-ion battery gets me into town and back on a single charge, without any pedaling. It helps us offset one of most country dwellers' biggest carbon contributors: their personal transportation.

Learning to live off the grid has been a tremendously challenging experience. I would never pretend there haven't been times of extreme frustration and anxiety. But getting over the speed bumps makes the times when things run smoothly all the more gratifying. On a cold winter night with a full moon, it's wonderful to skate on the pond and look back at the house to see the light beaming from the windows, using electricity that was created during the day by the sun or by the wind. The house is warm, heated by wood cut from our property and burned in an EPA-certified woodstove that ensures minimal emissions. And there's no feeling like pulling a wagon full of vegetables from the garden late in the summer, knowing that much of it will be stored in our root cellar or freezer and will keep our stomachs full all winter.

A few generations ago, this is how many Americans lived. Today, most of us have traded our independence to pay someone else to keep our homes warm, keep our lights on and keep our stomachs full. I think this is becoming an increasingly unstable proposition.

The technology exists for us to reduce our impact on the planet, and at the same time make us more independent and resilient to the shocks coming our way—and you don't have to live in the country to do it. Don't wait. Pick up a shovel and get started on a garden. Pick up a phone and call a solar dealer. Pick up that stack of credit card bills and vow to pay them off and stay out of debt. The rewards are infinite. Peace of mind comes from independence.

Organizations to Contact

The editors have compiled the following list of organizations concerned with the issues debated in this book. The descriptions are derived from materials provided by the organizations. All have publications or information available for interested readers. The list was compiled on the date of publication of the present volume; the information provided here may change. Be aware that many organizations take several weeks or longer to respond to inquiries, so allow as much time as possible.

Edison Electric Institute (EEI)
701 Pennsylvania Ave., NW, Washington, DC 20004-2696
(202) 508-5000
e-mail: feedback@eei.org
website: www.eei.org

EEI is a membership organization comprised of US shareholder-owned electric companies, which provide the majority of electricity to consumers in the United States. The institute advocates for legislative and regulatory policies that align with its members' interests. It also provides information about the industry to the public as well as policy makers. EEI government testimony, policy briefs, and articles from the institute's bimonthly magazine *Electric Perspectives* can be read online.

Electric Power Research Institute (EPRI)
3420 Hillview Ave., Palo Alto, CA 94304
(800) 313-3774 • (650) 855-2121
e-mail: askepri@apri.com
website: www.epri.com

EPRI is an independent non-profit organization dedicated to researching and improving electricity generation, delivery and use. Specific issues tackled by the institute's researchers include reliability, efficiency, health, safety, nuclear power, and the environment. Extensive information about these areas can be found on the EPRI website in the form of research papers and topical newsletters.

Federal Energy Regulatory Commission (FERC)
888 First St., NE, Washington, DC 20426
(866) 208-3372 • fax: (202) 502-6088
e-mail: customer@ferc.gov
website: www.ferc.gov

FERC is the federal government commission in charge of creating and enforcing regulations for interstate energy transmission to ensure that consumers have access to reliable, efficient, and sustainable energy at an appropriate cost. As the country continues to move toward the creation and implementation of a national smart grid, FERC has focused on making sure that this technology is secure, reliable, and beneficial to consumers nationwide. General information about smart grid regulations and grid security can be found on the FERC website.

Global Energy Network Institute (GENI)
1088 Third Ave., San Diego, CA 92101
(619) 595-0139 • fax: (619) 595-0403
e-mail: info@geni.org
website: www.geni.org

GENI seeks to inform the public and policy makers worldwide about the interconnected nature of international electricity networks and the necessity of employing renewable energy sources to meet global energy needs. GENI contends that recognizing this interconnection and utilizing renewable sources of energy will help to limit conflicts, expand economies, and improve life and health for individuals around the world. The GENI library provides maps of energy grids in individual countries and articles and research about the importance of energy grids in transmitting energy from renewable sources.

Institute for the Analysis of Global Security (IAGS)
7811 Montrose Rd., Suite 505, Potomac, MD 20854

(866) 713-7527
e-mail: info@iags.org
website: www.iags.org

IAGS has been working since its founding in 2002 to increase public and governmental awareness about the link between energy and security and foster debate on issues surrounding this link that could lead to an increase in international energy security. In both its general research as well as in its bimonthly publication *Journal of Energy Security*, the IAGS has addressed smart grid security issues in articles such as "Combating Smart Grid Vulnerabilities," "The Security Vulnerabilities of Smart Grid," and "Making a Secure Smart Grid a Reality." These articles and others can be read on the organization's website.

Institute of Electrical and Electronics Engineers (IEEE)
2001 L St., NW, Suite 700, Washington, DC 20036-4910
(202) 785-0017 • fax: (202) 785-0835
e-mail: ieeeusa@ieee.org
website: www.ieee.org

IEEE is a professional association of individuals involved in technology-related fields with the goal of advancing technology to improve the lives of humans around the world. The IEEE Smart Grid site is dedicated to providing a range of information about smart grid developments and current research. The publication *IEEE Transactions on Smart Grid* provides current articles and discussion about smart grid topics. Additional smart grid articles such as "Startling Smart Grid Developments," "Saving Smart Meters from a Backlash," and "Obama Administration Unveils 21st Century Grid Vision," can be found in the IEEE publication *Spectrum*.

International Energy Agency (IEA)
9, Rue de la Federation, 75739 Paris Cedex 15
France
+33 1 40 57 65 00 • fax: +33 1 40 57 65 09
e-mail: info@iea.org
website: www.iea.org

Founded in the wake of the 1973–74 oil crisis, the IEA has been working for more than four decades to help its member countries develop policies that ensure energy security, economic development in the energy sector, environmental awareness, and international dialogue on energy-related issues. The United States is one of the agency's founding members. Information about the status of specific energy sources by country can be found on the IEA website including access to the newsletters *OPEN Energy Technology Bulletin, Monthly Oil Survey, Monthly Natural Gas Survey, Monthly Oil Prices Survey*, and *Monthly Electricity Survey.*

North American Electric Reliability Corporation (NERC)
116-390 Village Blvd., Princeton, NJ 08540-5721
(609) 452-8060 • fax: (609) 452-9550
website: www.nerc.com

NERC has been working since 1968 to implement guidelines for the bulk power system in North America to maintain a continuous power supply in the United States and Canada, with plans to expand to Mexico when the government there adopts the appropriate policies. Both the US Federal Energy Regulatory Commission and Canadian governmental authorities oversee the actions of this self-regulatory nongovernmental organization. Information about NERC standards, compliance, the energy grid, and critical infrastructure protection can be found on the corporation's website.

SmartGridNews.com (SGN)
15127 NE 24th, Suite 358, Redmond, WA 98052
(425) 336-1426
e-mail: info@smartgridnews.com
website: www.smartgridnews.com

SGN is a website providing comprehensive information and analysis of smart grid developments in the form of research papers, case studies, videos, and stimulus tools. SGN commentary gives industry experts the opportunity to voice their opinions on how to improve the smart grid in articles such as

"The Smart Grid's Missing Ingredient: Performance Feedback," "Smart Grid and Privacy: Should We Borrow a Page from Telephone Record Privacy Rules?" and "A Declaration of Energy Independence that Might Just Work?" Information about the technologies necessary to successfully establish and run the smart grid is available on the SGN website as well.

US Department of Energy (DOE)

1000 Independence Ave., SW, Washington, DC 20585
(202) 586-5000 • fax (202) 586-4403
e-mail: The.Secretary@hq.doe.gov
website: www.energy.gov

The DOE is the US government agency charged with helping to maintain American security and prosperity by finding innovative ways to tackle to the country's energy, environmental, and nuclear challenges. In order to fulfill this mission, the DOE seeks to establish the United States as a leader in clean energy technology development and implementation, foster scientific research and innovation, ensure nuclear safety and security, and provide the guidelines and planning necessary to achieve these goals. The DOE has an entire website dedicated to providing information about the smart grid with articles such as "Five Million Smart Meters Installed Nationwide Is Just the Beginning of Smart Grid Progress," and "Modernizing the Grid: Keeping the Dialogue Going." Information about the smart grid is also available on the DOE website smartgrid.gov.

Bibliography

Books

Robert U. Ayres and Edward H. Ayres	*Crossing the Energy Divide: Moving from Fossil Fuel Dependence to a Clean-Energy Future.* Upper Saddle River, NJ: Pearson, 2010.
David Black	*Living off the Grid: A Simple Guide to Creating and Maintaining a Self-reliant Supply of Energy, Water, Shelter and More.* New York: Skyhorse, 2008.
Daniel Botkin	*Powering the Future: A Scientist's Guide to Energy Independence.* Upper Saddle River, NJ: Pearson, 2010.
Robert Bryce	*Power Hungry: The Myths of "Green" Energy and the Real Fuels of the Future.* New York: PublicAffairs, 2010.
S. Chowdhury, S.P. Chowdhury, and P. Crossley	*Microgrids and Active Distribution Networks.* London, UK: Institution of Engineering and Technology, 2009.
Robert L. Evans	*Fueling Our Future: An Introduction to Sustainable Energy.* New York: Cambridge University Press, 2007.
Tony Flick and Justin Morehouse	*Securing the Smart Grid: Next Generation Power Grid Security.* New York: Syngress, 2011.

Peter Fox-Penner *Smart Power: Climate Change, the Smart Grid, and the Future of Electric Utilities*. Washington, DC: Island, 2010.

Robert Galvin and Kurt Yeager *Perfect Power: How the Microgrid Revolution Will Unleash Cleaner, Greener, More Abundant Energy*. New York: McGraw-Hill, 2009.

Clark W. Gellings *The Smart Grid: Enabling Energy Efficiency and Demand Response*. Lilburn, GA: Fairmont, 2009.

Stan Mark Kaplan, Fred Sissine, and The Capitol.Net *Smart Grid: Modernizing Electric Power Transmission and Distribution; Energy Independence, Storage and Security; Energy Independence and Security Act of 2007 (EISA); Improving Electrical Grid Efficiency, Communication, Reliability, and Resiliency; Integrating New and Renewable Energy Sources*. Alexandria, VA: The Capitol.Net, 2009.

David J.C. MacKay *Sustainable Energy—Without the Hot Air*. Cambridge, UK: UIT Cambridge, 2009.

Richard Munson *From Edison to Enron: The Business of Power and What It Means for the Future of Electricity*. Westport, CT: Praeger, 2005.

Bob Shivley and John Ferrare *Understanding Today's Electricity Business*. Laporte, CO: Enerdynamics, 2010.

Fereidoon P. Sioshansi, ed. — *Smart Grid: Integrating Renewable, Distributed & Efficient Energy*. New York: Academic, 2011.

Periodicals and Internet Sources

Frank Andorka — "Powering Up: The Smart Grid's Next Steps," *IW (Industry Week)*, May 2011.

David P. Chassin — "What Can the Smart Grid Do for You? And What Can You Do for the Smart Grid?" *Electricity Journal*, June 2010.

Sean Davies — "Internet of Energy," *Engineering & Technology*, October 23, 2010.

Economist — "Building the Smart Grid," June 6, 2009.

Randy Frank — "Electric Vehicles: The Smart Grid's Moving Target," *Electronic Design*, June 17, 2010.

Jennifer Ginn — "How Many Jobs Is Smart Grid Creating?" *Capitol Ideas*, May/June 2010.

Alison C. Graab — "The Smart Grid: A Smart Solution to a Complicated Problem," *William & Mary Law Review*, May 2011.

Dave Greenfield — "Is the Smart Grid a Dumb Idea?" *eWeek*, November 9, 2009.

Melissa Hathaway — "Power Hackers," *Scientific American*, October 2010.

Ryan Hledik	"How Green Is the Smart Grid?" *Electricity Journal*, April 2009.
Brian Fisher Johnson	"Making Electric Grids Smarter," *Earth*, May 2009.
David Kramer	"'Smart Grid' Gets Big Stimulus from US Recovery Plan," *Physics Today*, April 2009.
Marc Levinson	"Is the Smart Grid Really a Smart Idea?" *Issues in Science & Technology*, Fall 2010.
David Lindley	"Smart Grids: The Energy Storage Problem," *Nature*, January 7, 2010.
Lawrence J. Makovich	"The Smart Grid Separating Perception from Reality," *Issues in Science & Technology*, Spring 2011.
Emma Marris	"Energy: Upgrading the Grid," *Nature*, July 31, 2008.
Mike Martin	"The Great Green Grid," *E: The Environmental Magazine*, July/August 2010.
Jeremy P. Meyers	"Lightning in a Bottle: Storing Energy for the 'Smart Grid,'" *Interface*, Fall 2010.
Noreen Parks	"Energy Efficiency and the Smart Grid," *Environmental Science & Technology*, May 1, 2009.
Alex Pavlak	"Wind Energy Contribution to a Low-Carbon Grid," *Electricity Journal*, May 2010.

Gail Reitenbach — "The Smart Grid and Distributed Generation: Better Together," *Power*, April 2011.

Ahmed Yousuf Saber and Ganesh Kumar Venayagamoorthy — "Plug-in Vehicles and Renewable Energy Sources for Cost and Emission Reductions," *IEEE Transactions on Industrial Electronics*, April 1, 2011.

Mesa Scharf — "Bringing Solar Power to the Smart Grid," *Power Engineering*, May 2010.

Bridget Mintz Testa — "Building the New Electric Grid," *Mechanical Engineering*, December 2009.

Index

D

E

F

G

H

I

J

K

L

M

N

O

P

T

U

V

W

X